The Neglected Dimension
Ethnicity in American Life

The Neglected Dimension
Ethnicity in American Life

PHILIP ROSEN

UNIVERSITY OF NOTRE DAME PRESS
NOTRE DAME – LONDON

This work was developed under a grant from the U.S. Office of Education,
Department of Health, Education, and Welfare. However, the content does not
necessarily reflect the position or policy of that Agency, and no official endorsement of these materials should be inferred.

Library of Congress Cataloging in Publication Data

Rosen, Philip, 1928–
  The neglected dimension.
  Includes index.
  1. United States—Social conditions—1960–
2. Ethnicity. 3. Ethnic groups. 4. Ethnology—
United States. I. Title
HN59.R66   301.45′1′0973   79-13111
ISBN O-268-01451-5
ISBN O-268-01452-3 pbk.

Manufactured in the United States of America

Contents

Foreword

If American education is going to begin to prepare students and adults to live together in our ethnically, racially, and culturally diverse society, then the curriculum of our schools must reflect that diversity. Students must be provided with opportunities to perceive their own heritage as legitimate. They must get in touch with their own stories and experiences.

The Ethnic Heritage Studies Program, Title IX of the Elementary and Secondary Education Act, was designed to "afford students opportunities to learn more about the nature of their own heritage and to study the contributions of the cultural heritage of other ethnic groups." Monsignor Geno Baroni, founder of the National Center for Urban Ethnic Affairs (NCUEA), initiated the development of wholesome approaches to ethnicity. Funding from the Ford Foundation and the U.S. Office of Education resulted in the creation of new educational materials and models. These materials are presented in this volume.

It is the hope of the NCUEA that this book will assist students, parents, and teachers by providing fuller understanding of diversity in America so that liberty and justice will prevail in our land.

John A. Kromkowski
President
The National Center for
Urban Ethnic Affairs

Preface to the Student

You are about to study a field of social science largely ignored in school—ethnic groups and ethnicity. These terms have different meanings to various writers. To some, ethnic groups are blacks, Orientals such as Chinese and Japanese, American Indians, and Hispanic Americans, such as Mexican Americans and Puerto Ricans. They are characterized as *minorities,* peoples who do not have the advantages and opportunities afforded other Americans. To others, ethnic groups are immigrants and their immediate descendants living apart in separate ''colonies'' in the city or country, still speaking a foreign tongue, and practicing quaint customs. A few writers think of ''ethnics'' simply as Americans descended from Central, Eastern, or Southern Europe.

This study defines ethnic groups as a people bound together by ties of common religion (such as Catholics, Lutherans, or Mormons), or by ties of race (as are blacks and American Indians), or by ties of national origin (such as Italian Americans, Polish Americans, or Irish Americans). Ethnic groups often combine two or more of these factors.

Included in this definition are the majority of the American population: white Protestants. They are found among groups of people with distinctive backgrounds and customs. Those descended from Great Britain can be subdivided into English, Scotch, and Welsh. These ''charter group'' founders of the United States were joined by immigrants from Scandinavia, Netherlands, and Germany who intermarried and mingled widely with the British stock. Their descendants form part of the Protestant majority.

A geographic component makes for additional ethnic differences. The Protestant from Appalachia, the ''Hillbilly,'' is vastly different from the Yankee blue blood living near Boston. Perhaps

the common denominator of any ethnic group is their shared historical origin and their experiences in America.

Ethnicity is a term writers can agree upon. It means human
behavior growing out of belonging to an ethnic group. It is also the
behavior of the group itself. Some of you reading this may not
identify with an ethnic group or only identify weakly. You may
think your decisions are individual. This book contends that individual choice is greatly influenced by subtle ethnic factors operating
both consciously and subconsciously upon people. You will receive
evidence of how ethnicity expresses itself in many areas of individual choice—neighborhood, organizational activity, political
party, political candidate, and opinions on crucial issues of public
policy.

Why is ethnicity dubbed a "neglected dimension?" Many
writers on American society do not point out the part played by
ethnic groups and ethnicity. There are a number of reasons for this.
Most define the field merely in terms of minority-majority relations,
often black-white relations, with the whites homogenized like milk.
They fail to differentiate the many cultural variations within white
society. They hold the view that in America distinctive ethnic
groups lose their features, similar systems of education and communication wipe out differences. America is a melting pot. These
social scientists stress class factors, behavior based on a person's
position in society determined by his or her occupation, income,
wealth, and education. Furthermore, they suspect ethnicity as a
source of prejudice, discrimination, and conflict. They prefer uni-
versalism, stressing human sameness, not diversity. With this mental set, their writings tend to ignore or play down ethnicity.

This study sets out with a hypothesis that we are all members
of one ethnic group or another, and that ethnicity is a major factor in
American life, explaining a great deal of social and political behavior. The learning experiences are designed to prove that hypothesis.
Many groups are used to illustrate principles of ethnicity.

What good are such learning experiences? Most important they
make you aware of this neglected dimension. By learning about the
nature and behavior of ethnic groups you will become more self-
conscious. You will understand some of the motives behind your
and your family's behavior. By understanding ethnicity you should

develop a greater appreciation for other groups. To know what it is to be a Polish American or Italian American is to gain insight of what Afro-Americans are about. If you are black or from a non-white group, you will realize that white society has many subdivisions, some of which are building their own group awareness. Such a study should increase your understanding of public issues, for a number of them have ethnic overtones.

The purpose of this study is not only to provide you with information but to use that information as a means to get at your attitudes and values. You will be introduced to a problem, asked to explore alternate solutions, then make up your own mind.

The aim of the learning experiences is not to indoctrinate. If you complete the course convinced that you do not wish to identify strongly with one group that is fine. If you do not change your mind on a number of ethnic related issues, hopefully, you will be better able to defend your position with evidence and argument. You may even reject the hypothesis of the study; the conclusion offers an opposing view. That, too, is part of learning that conclusions in social science are controversial and subject to change in the light of evidence. This work, unlike so many student materials, does not assert its conclusions as absolute truth. It offers to share experiences with you and encourage you to test its findings.

Ethnicity and Our Identity

In this course there are thirty-four topics which are presented in the form of questions or problems. You will be asked to hypothesize, that is, give a temporary answer in the form of a statement to the question. For each topic there are introductions which provide you with background information helpful in understanding the data (information) that follow. Included are some pointed questions that aid you to get at principles of ethnic behavior. Listen carefully in class and take notes on class discussion and on the readings and other material presented. The learning experiences provided by each topic lead to conclusions, answers to the large question posed in the topic and smaller ones found in the introductions. Take an active role in trying to learn what is set out and volunteer for enrichment activities.

The topics are clustered about themes, which are generalizations that pull the ideas found in the learning experiences together and organize them. Theme One is the concept that ethnicity is a measure of self-identity. There are many ways to identify. You may say: I am a student, football player, debater, attractive person, math major, good son/daughter, club president, and so on. Topics 1 and 2 provide learning experiences which ask you to think of your identity in terms of race, religion, country of ancestors, your acceptance of others, and your views on ethnic-related issues. Yes, your opinions on issues help define you.

What is in a name? Plenty! One can mark you for life. Topics 3 and 4 illustrate how a name becomes an important part of one's identity. The first name and last name reveals how you (and your parents) identify with groups and aids others in identifying you.

Theme Two states that America is made up of ethnic groups. The American people include nearly every nationality, race, and creed in the world. Since statistics were taken on immigration from 1820 on, over forty-five million newcomers found homes here. It was the influx of many national populations that became the basis for present-day ethnic groups. Topic 5 provides you with the opportunity to guess at the ethnic makeup of the American people. The momentous saga of immigration and adjustment in the United States receives only cursory treatment in most school textbooks. Topic 6 offers in evidence some typical passages which leave misleading impressions. You may compare notes of your analysis of these passages with the description in Topic 7. The latter topic also provides an orientation to the remainder of the course.

Ethnicity Is a Measure of Self-Identity

These American children are dressed to celebrate a Polish festival. How does this help them become more aware of their own identity as members of an ethnic group?

Who Am I – How Do I Feel about Others?

With the help of your parents and an exploration of your own feelings answer the questions below. Try to answer as many as you can as honestly as you can since class discussion will be based on the answers. The information will give the class an idea of the diverse backgrounds in our room and provide ideas that will be employed later. You may choose to eliminate some questions for personal reasons.

1. Who was the first member of your family to immigrate to America? (Yourself, parent(s), grandparent(s), great grandparent(s), or earlier ancestor) Specify which member.

2. Tell country(s) from which you or your parents, grandparents, or ancestors came. Specify who came from where.

3. Does anyone in your family still speak the language of a country of origin (the country from which they came) or a language of folk living in a foreign land? Specify who speaks what language.

4. Do you or any of your relatives keep in touch with relations or friends in country(s) of origin or some other foreign country?

5. With which religion (sect or denomination) do you identify?

6. How strongly do you identify with this religion? (Very strongly, fairly strongly, moderately, in name only)

7. Of which national origins group do you feel a part? (Afro-American, Irish-American, Polish-American, British-American, etc., mixed, no particular group)

8. Place the following terms of identity in the circles according to which category is closest to yourself:
   American
   national origin (English, Irish, German, Puerto Rican, etc.)
   religion (Protestant, Catholic, Jewish, etc.)
   race (white, black, Mongoloid [Asiatic], other)

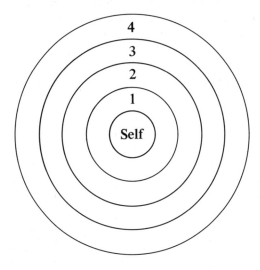

9. What interest do you have in the history and culture of your national origins group? (Great interest, moderate interest, a little interest, no interest)

10. What interest do you have in your religious group? (Great, moderate, little, none)

HOW DO I FEEL ABOUT OTHERS?—A SOCIAL-DISTANCE SCALE

A social-distance scale measures how close we feel toward others and how much we accept them. In our acceptance and rejection of others we define ourselves. This scale is anonymous; do not sign your name; merely provide the requested information concerning yourself on the first group of lines below. Please give your first feeling reactions in every case. Mark each group even though you have had no contact with the group. Check as many of the six columns as your feelings dictate.

race	religion		national origin group			sex
American ethnic group	*Would marry*	*Would date*	*Have as close friend*	*Have as next-door neighbor*	*Have speaking acquaintance with*	*Have in same school*
Arab						
Armenian						
Catholic						
Chinese						
Czech						
English						
French						
German						
Greek						

Indian					
Irish					
Italian					
Japanese					
Jewish					
Mexican					
Norwegian					
blacks					
Polish					
Protestant					
Puerto Rican					
others (as suggested)					

What Are My Opinions
on Ethnic-Related Issues?

This questionnaire concerns issues which have a strong relationship to how you view your own ethnicity. It serves primarily for
self-examination, and its results will not be part of your grade. The
questions asked are ones with which you will be confronted time
and again throughout your life. Because they test your beliefs, there
are no right or wrong answers, so feel free to answer honestly, not
according to how you think your teacher or someone else wants.

At the conclusion of this course you will receive the same
questionnaire to measure whether you have changed your mind on
the issues raised by these questions. The thirty-two topics that follow provide information that will help you think more deeply about
ethnic-related issues. If at the end you answer the same as you do
here in the beginning, we hope you will have more evidence and
developed reasons to support your views. Likewise, if you change
your mind, it will be interesting to note why.

Examine the questionnaire closely. After completion your
teacher may call on you to justify your answers. *Note the important
decisions in which the ethnic factor plays a part. What relationship
does this questionnaire have with the previous one?*

ATTITUDE QUESTIONNAIRE ON ETHNIC ISSUES*

data	name	section

Directions: This questionnaire seeks your opinions or beliefs and cannot fairly be recorded as part of your grades. Please answer with complete honesty. Place a check mark in the space provided next to the letter of the statement that comes closest to your view on each issue or topic. If no statement is acceptable, write in the space provided at D an original statement or reword a statement from A, B, or C which does express your view.

1. *Ethnic Neighborhoods*

_____A. Neighborhoods should be integrated with people of all different backgrounds to promote good intergroup relations and break down artificial divisions in American society.

_____B. Neighborhood preference is a matter of personal choice; clustering into neighborhoods by members of the same ethnic group is acceptable so long as there are no secret agreements to keep out members of other ethnic groups.

_____C. People are better off living in neighborhoods with their own kind; they feel comfortable and avoid interethnic conflict.

_____ Other: _____
_____
_____

2. *"Foreign-Sounding" Names*

_____A. A person with such a name should change it to an American-sounding one; he or she is living in America now.

*Composed by Philip Rosen, instructor in history, Northeast High School, Philadelphia, PA, 1972.

———B. Names are a means of identity; a person should not feel embarrassed if he or she keeps or changes his name.

———C. A person should have pride in his or her name, for it is inherited as a birthright. If people have trouble in pronouncing or spelling the name, the person should take care to explain it to them.

———D. Other: ————————————————————

————————————————————

————————————————————

3. *Friendship Groups*

———A. Choosing friends on the basis of similar ethnic background threatens good group relations and divides our country. People should seek interethnic associations.

———B. An individual should feel free, without a sense of guilt, to choose friends within his own ethnic group, or seek multiethnic contacts, or even change his ethnic identification if he desires.

———C. People are better off, more comfortable, and safer when they stay within the bounds of their own ethnic group. They should seek friends from their own kind.

———D. Other: ————————————————————

————————————————————

————————————————————

4. *Joining a Fraternity or Sorority*

———A. Fraternities and sororities should be multiethnic so that the membership can learn to get along with all kinds of people.

———B. Fraternities and sororities which do not have as their goal the preservation of religious or nationality values should be made open to all; those that are ethnically sponsored may place ethnic criteria for membership.

_____C. People should feel free to set up criteria in their social organizations any way they choose; this includes ethnic criteria.

_____D. Other: _____

_____

_____

5. *Interethnic Marriage*

_____A. Interethnic marriages are a good way to break down barriers between people and bring about a united America.

_____B. Interethnic marriages are a private affair between the couple involved, a matter of free choice if ethnic references mean little to them.

_____C. People are better off marrying within their own ethnic group; there are enough potentially good mates within one's own group.

_____D. Other: _____

_____

_____

6. *Voting for an Ethnic Candidate*

_____A. One should vote for the best candidate and not consider at all the candidate's ethnic background.

_____B. A voter who votes for a candidate from the same ethnic group as himself may be making sense if the candidate is qualified and takes a position that would serve the best interests of the voter and the group to which he belongs.

_____C. A voter should prefer a candidate from his own ethnic group since it is more likely that a candidate once in office would look out after the interests of the ethnic group.

_____D. Other: _____

_____

_____

7. *Ethnic Considerations for Appointments to Public Office*
   (Judges, etc.)

_____A. The choice of a person for a public office should rest solely on merit. Ethnic considerations are irrelevant.

_____B. Ethnic considerations do make sense when a large ethnic population resides in a voting area, yet has no representation in important governmental bodies.

_____C. An ethnic group should have the exact proportion of representatives in governmental bodies as its numbers in the voting population would indicate.

_____D. Other: _____
_____
_____
_____

8. *Other-Nation Loyalties: Concern for Peoples outside the United States*

_____A. Concern with brethren overseas is narrow. One should be concerned with all people, how they are treated and whether they are suffering, not only with those with whom there are historic nationality ties.

_____B. Concern for overseas brethren seems natural, but the makers of foreign policy have to be guided by the self-interests of the nation, not the concerns of one group.

_____C. Americans who have historic ties to brethren overseas are the people who naturally will show the most concern. Exerting pressure on government officials is a democratic right of all Americans, and a democratic government which professes concern over the desires of its citizens must modify its foreign policy accordingly.

_____D. Other: _____
_____
_____
_____

9. *Aid to Religious Schools*

_____A. Religious schools help to separate people and prevent interethnic contact that makes for good human relations. All children should go to public schools.

_____B. Religious schools are a democratic right, part of the exercise of religious freedom, but they should be financed by their subscribers, not public funds.

_____C. Parents should not be penalized for exercising their right to send their children to religious schools. Since these schools meet educational standards set by the state and provide the community's young people with a useful education, they should be financed by public funds.

_____D. Other: _____

_____

_____

_____

Why Can't He Change His Name?

A comedian made these remarks before a nightclub audience:

"As the space capsule began to enter the earth's atmosphere, Captain John Armstrong fired the retro-rockets."

"As the space capsule began to enter the earth's atmosphere, Captain Chester Chybrzynski fired the retro-rockets" (laughter)

Why did the second statement evoke laughter in the audience? Could it have something to do with stereotypes? Read this article by Mike Royko about famous boxers. What relationship does the name change have with the laughter in the second statement? Do you agree with Royko's conclusion? If not, can you offer another one?

Ali Boxed In by Name Game

Mike Royko

The world of sports experts is still split over what to call Muhammad Ali.

Most of them insist that his name is Cassius Clay, because that is what he was born and that is what they are going to call him.

Others get cute and call him Ali (nee Clay), and some lump the two names together and make him Ali-Clay.

Mike Royko column, reprinted with permission from the March 4, 1971, *Chicago Daily News.*

Muhammad Ali. Why would he change his name from Cassius Clay? Courtesy Wide World Photos.

Only a few respect his request to be known as Muhammad Ali, a name he has chosen because of his affiliation with the Muslim religion.

The night that Rocky Marciano beat Joe Louis none of them insisted on writing that Rocco Francis Marchegiano defeated Joe L. Barrow, the names the fighters were born with.

And when Arnold Raymond Cream preferred another name the sports writers gladly went along. So he became known as Jersey Joe Walcott, another heavyweight champ.

Oldtimers will have trouble identifying Joseph P. Zukauskas. He became heavyweight champ as Jack Sharkey.

Dropping down to the light heavyweight division, does anyone remember that great title bout in 1952 when Archibald Lee Wright beat Guiseppe Antonio Bernardinelli? Probably not, because the headlines said: ''Archie Moore whips Joey Maxim.''

In fact, prizefighters have been almost as quick to change their names as are movie stars, and until Clay came along nobody made a fuss out of it.

Among past middleweight champions there have been Stanislaus Kiecal (Stanley Ketchel), George Chipulonis (George Chip), Al Rudolph (Al McCoy), John Panica (Johnny Wilson), Morris Jaboltowski (Ben Jeby), Vincent Lazzaro (Vince Dundee) and Henry Pylkowski (Eddie Risko).

For real brawlers, though, you couldn't ask for more than the three legendary fights between Rocco Barbella (Rocky Graziano) and Anthony Florian Zaleski (Tony Zale).

Neither of them, however, were a match for the fighter many people consider to be the greatest of all time—the one and only Walker Smith.

You don't remember the one and only Walker Smith?

That's because he preferred being known as Sugar Ray Robinson, and the sports writers didn't get petulant about it.

There were some fine welterweight champs who underwent name-changes, too.

In the 20s, Joe Dundee (born Sam Lazzaro) was beaten in a title bout by Jackie Fields (born Jacob Finklestein).

In the 30s, Young Corbett won the title. He was born Ralph Giordano.

And the fight buffs still talk about the night that Henry Jackson fought and won the title from tough Barnet Rosofsky. Who? They went under the names Henry Armstrong and Barney Ross.

In the late 40s and early 50s, the top welterweight was somebody born Gerardo Gonzalez. He became famous as Kid Gavilan.

There was a time when hardly any lightweight champion used his real name.

In the 20s, Benny Leonard (born Benjamin Leiner) was succeeded by Jimmy Goodrich (born James E. Moran), who was beaten by Rocky Kansas (born Rocco Tozzo), and he was beaten by Sammy Mandell (born Samuel Mandella).

In the 30s, there was Lou Ambers (born Louis D'Ambrosio). Then you had Lew Jenkins (born Verlin Jenks), and he lost to Sammy Angott (born Samuel Engotti), who was succeeded by Beau Jack (born Sidney Walker).

And the greatest featherweight of them all may have been that long-time champion William Guiglermo Papaleo.

Huh?

Try Willie Pep.

I suspect that most sports writers merely reflect public opinion. They dislike Ali for most of the reasons that the majority of people dislike him. Arrogance, his draft situation, his Muslim connections and his big mouth.

They preferred someone like sweet, lovable Joe Louis (nee Joe L. Barrow), because he was a good white's black man, respectful, grateful and never stepping out of line in word or deed.

This good conduct got him fleeced by his advisors, plucked by the tax people, and helped put him in a mental hospital.

So if they can't poke Ali in his pretty face, they can get in a jab by refusing to extend the courtesy of using the name of his choice.

And that is why Joe Frazier finds himself in a strange position for a black man in 1971.

Frazier has become, of all things, The Great White Hope.

TOPIC 4

What's in a Name?

Selection 1

The following excerpt is from a paper by Evelyn Hersey, ''The Emotional Conflicts of the Second-Generation: A Discussion of American-Born Children of Immigrant Parents.'' It was presented at a meeting of the National Conference of Social Work, May 21, 1934. Does it have any relevance today? Did anyone in your family have a similar experience?

Many firms refuse to employ girls whose names end in 's-k-y', and a bank reported recently that they had to discharge a very able young man because he ''looked so foreign'' the patrons objected. Some of these second generation young people come to a definite decision to deny their background. I once asked a very successful prominent caterer whom I knew to be Czech why he had changed his name to Alden. ''Economic necessity. The elite of this city would not trade with a man with a Slavic name. I tried it.'' ''Don't the old folks mind your losing the family name?'' A shadow passed over his face as he answered, ''It nearly killed my father, but he sees now it was necessary.'' It is to these experiences that we owe numbers of Bakers, Smiths, Davis's and Cabots in the Polish, Czech, Hungarian and Italian communities.

Selection 2

I find I have a problem introducing my parents to my friends and others because they speak with heavy accents and in bro-

18

ken English. I am particularly embarrassed when I date, for I am afraid I lose status when a boy meets my mom or dad. I avoid having them come to school to meet my teachers because I am afraid they will not understand the ways of the American school system. It is also humiliating to have the teacher and my classmates stumble over my foreign-sounding name. I have arranged to have my teachers and friends call me by a nickname.

What would be the consequences if all children of immigrants felt this way? In what ways are you different than your parents?

Selection 3

I am proud that my parents are Spanish immigrants. We are descended from a people that have a rich and civilized culture. Spain once ruled a great empire and was the world's foremost nation. My first name is after my uncle, a learned and fine man. My second name is my mother's family name, and my last name is the same as one of Spain's greatest writers. I make sure my teachers and friends know how to pronounce my name.

What would be the consequences if all children of immigrants felt this way? What is your attitude to those who are different?

Selection 4

A first name and, to a greater degree, a last name give a person identity. A name like Muhammad reveals a connection with the Arab-Moslem world, for it is the name of the founder of Islam. A name ending in *ski,* as in Stanislawski, is the Polish equivalent of ''son of.'' Stanislaw was a famous Polish hero. Rosenwald is a name taken from the German words for roses and forest. Read the following selection taken from the *Pitt Magazine,* based on the *Pitt Student Directory. What reason is offered for a name change? Can you think of other names that fit these nationalities? List some other ethnic groups and common surnames. Do you agree that "names . . . reflect with remarkable clarity the mixture of clans, tribes, and families who emigrated from all over the world to settle America." Why or why not?*

What's in a Name?

Curious as to the ethnic makeup of the University of Pittsburgh student body, and lacking data to draw upon, we asked the committees which built the Nationality Rooms to examine the 7,500 names in the 1972–3 *Pitt Student Directory* and identify those which seem to indicate a national origin.

Much more thorough research would be needed to discover how often Petropoulos became Peterson or Davidowich was transformed to Davis with a flick of the pen at Ellis Island or later by personal choice. A change of name often makes life less complicated in an American society limited by its near total dependence on the English language as a means of recognition and communication.

A scan of the *Directory* indicates that thousands of Pitt students carry their ancestors' names, which reflect with remarkable clarity the mixture of clans, tribes, and families who emigrated from all over the world to settle America.

Reprinted with permission from *Pitt*, vol. 29, no. 2(Summer 1973).

Nationality	Total	*Samples of names found in* Pitt Student Directory *(from 7,500 listed)*
Chinese	48	Chang, Lee, Lim, Oh, Pong, Wong, Wu, Yee
Czechoslovak	139	Bilohlavek, Buchko, Drobny, Janasek, Kacmar
English	796	Allen, Barker, Clark, Cook, Hall, Hill, Miller, Taylor
French	96	Beaumont, Belle, Bourgue, Carabin, Delong, Faux
German	1,115	Ackermann, Brittenbaugh, Dietrich, Eichenlaub, Froehlich
Greek	28	Antinopoulos, Apostolakis, Karnavas, Kladitis, Pallas
Hungarian	130	Bacsi, Bardos, Dudash, Hadjuk, Horvat, Kovaks, Novak
Irish	646	Ahearn, Brannigan, Callahan, Gleason, Hurley, Maloney, O'Neill
Italian	812	Adonzio, Baccelli, DeAngelis, Francellini, Gentile, Nardo
Lithuanian	18	Abramitis, Dudemas, Kaleida, Miskinis, Shukis, Toaras
Norwegian	13	Berg, Hansen, Larsen, Slomberg, Slota, Strandberg, Strom
Polish	316	Bajkowski, Bednarek, Chybrzyn-ski, Matuszak, Sapolsky
Russian	158	Alexeief, Ekimoff, Fetcenko, Ivanoff, Krushin, Tabachnik
Scottish	410	Andrews, Baird, Beatty, Lang, McFeaters, Scott, Stewart
Swedish	70	Anderson, Freeberg, Holmquist, Persson, Peterson, Uhlmann
Yugoslav	196	Bosiljevac, Bradjic, Gluscic, Javonovich, Pavlovich
Syrian Lebanese (or other Arab)	9	Bitar, Demir, Khalill, Khouri, Muhamed, Salehizadeh, Sulaiman

The American People as Ethnic Groups

Shopping from street vendors in a New York City ethnic neighborhood in 1898. Courtesy Museum of the City of New York.

Who Makes Up America?

The United States is a nation of immigrants. Even the original inhabitants of this land, the Indians, migrated to its shores thousands of years ago from Asia. Today Americans trace their ancestry to almost all the nations and continents of this planet.

The first census in 1790 recorded one out of every five Americans as black. Of the total population of 3.9 million in 1790 over 90 percent of the whites were of British descent, while 98 percent were Protestant. For most of our history the white, Anglo-Saxon (of British descent), Protestant, native-born American of native-born parents has been viewed as the "American majority," even though millions of immigrants from many nations came to our shores. The next three topics deal with the nature of the American population and how textbooks tend to present Americans.

Is there any one national origins group that constitutes an American majority today? The chart and graphs below provide the principal sources of immigration to the United States during the period 1820–1966. The first immigrants at Jamestown, Virginia, or the Pilgrims at Plymouth, Massachusetts, in the 1600s are not included because collection of immigration statistics did not begin until 1820. It also does not include the Spanish when the United States annexed Florida in 1819, or the Mexicans who came under the United States flag after the war with Mexico in 1848. *What does this data suggest about the national origins of present-day Americans? Is there a clear-cut ethnic majority today?*

IMMIGRATION TO THE UNITED STATES: 1820–1966

Country of last permanent residence	Total immigration
Germany	6,862,900
Italy	5,067,717
Great Britain	4,711,711
Ireland	4,706,854
Canada	3,836,071
U.S.S.R.	3,345,610
Mexico	1,414,273
Sweden	1,261,768
Norway	849,811
West Indies	777,382
France	713,532
Greece	514,700
Poland	473,670
China	419,643
South America	400,926
Turkey	370,827
Denmark	357,342
Japan	348,623
Netherlands	345,036
Switzerland	335,818
Portugal	305,844
Spain	201,916
Belgium	195,319
Romania	160,459
Czechoslovakia	130,569

Compiled from U.S. Bureau of Census, *Statistical Abstract,* 1967.

IMMIGRANTS TO THE UNITED STATES: 1820-1970
PIE GRAPHS

These pie graphs give you an idea of the numbers of Americans descended from different large regions of the globe. Note the different slices (fractions or percent) and how they change for each time period.

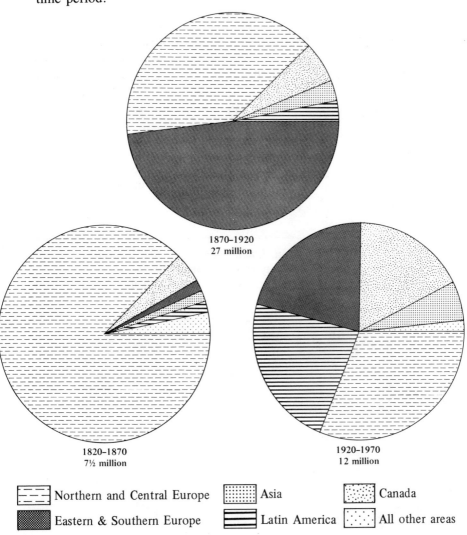

1870-1920
27 million

1820-1870
7½ million

1920-1970
12 million

Northern and Central Europe   Asia   Canada

Eastern & Southern Europe   Latin America   All other areas

What do the chart and graphs suggest about the national origins of present-day Americans? Look on a world map for the countries that comprise the regions in the above graphs. Check your guesses about national origins against some Census Bureau data which will be given to you.

TABLE A

PERCENT DISTRIBUTION OF ETHNIC GROUPS BY RELIGION

Father's background*	Protestant	Catholic	Jewish
black	94	6	0
Eastern European	13	59	28
English	68	31	1
German	51	36	13
Irish	17	83	0
Italian	2	98	0
Polish	5	82	13
Spanish-speaking	11	89	0

Source: Harold J. Abramson, *Ethnic Pluralism in the Connecticut Central City* (Storrs, Conn.: University of Connecticut, 1971).
*Determined by how interviewee defined himself, whether American-born or not.

STUDY SHEET

ESTIMATES OF UNITED STATES POPULATION

Protestant	_____%
Catholic	_____%
Jewish	_____%
Eastern Orthodox	_____%
whites	_____%
blacks	_____%
Oriental	_____%
Spanish origin (Puerto Rican, Mexican, etc.)	_____%
British	_____%
German	_____%
Irish	_____%
Italian	_____%
Polish	_____%
Russian	_____%
others	_____%

What Do Textbooks Say about the Ethnic Groups That Make Up the American People?

After you examine statistics about who Americans are, some questions may arise: What has been the impact of these immigrants on American society? What has been the impact of American society on them? The following passages from widely used textbooks tell about immigration and the peoples who make up America. *What picture do these excerpts give of the role of the immigrant in the United States? What do they suggest happened to the sons and daughters and the grandchildren of the immigrants?*

Give me your tired, your poor,
Your huddled masses yearning to breathe free,
The wretched refuse of your teeming shore . . .

> Portion of poem by Emma Lazarus engraved on Statue of Liberty and quoted widely in American history texts.

*   *   *   *   *

The changing character of immigration, as well as the swelling tide, alarmed many American. Down to the early 1880's the largest number of immigrants came from northwestern Europe—from Great Britain, Ireland, Scandinavia, Germany, and the Netherlands. But after 1890 an increasingly large number came from southern and eastern Europe. The languages, customs, and ways of living of these immigrants were quite different from those of immigrants from northwestern Europe. . . .

The great number of immigrants had an enormous influence on American life. Although some of the newcomers settled on farms, the great majority moved to the densely crowded slum areas of the cities. Here they competed with established residents for housing, thereby driving up rents and real estate prices.

Most immediate of all, however, was their effect upon American workers. They competed with American wage earners for jobs, thereby driving down the existing scale of wages. To be sure, immigrants helped to stimulate the economy by creating new demands for factory and farm products. But the average wage earner was more disturbed by the job competition of the immigrants than he was impressed with the stimulating effects of large-scale immigration.

> From secondary text, Lewis Paul Todd and Merle Curti, *The Rise of the American Nation* (New York: Harcourt, Brace, Jovanovitch, Inc., 1972), p. 499.

*   *   *   *   *

They [northern Europeans] spoke English or learned it quickly. Soon they lived much like their new American neighbors . . . . New immigrants came from Southern and Eastern Europe. Instead of adopting the language and customs of older Americans, they moved into neighborhoods of their own. "Little Italys" and "Little Polands" grew up as towns within big cities. Russians, Poles, Slavs, Greeks, and Italians continued to speak their native languages and follow old country customs.

> From secondary text, Margaret Branson and Edward French, *American History for Today* (Boston: Ginn and Co., 1970), p. 328.

*   *   *   *   *

What is an American? Almost no American (except the Indians) can trace his ancestors in this country back beyond the 1600's. Most of us would find that our ancestors came to North America much later, probably in the 1800's or perhaps in the 1900's. For America is a nation of immigrants or descendants of immigrants, whether our forefathers came to the New World in colonial days or in the years of great migrations or later. Americans today, therefore, are a mix of nationalities. We believe that America has blended the best features of many peoples to produce a vigorous new national stock. Dorothy Thompson, a well-known writer, gave us a humorous description of the American nationality: "What is an American?—An American is a fellow whose grandfather was·a German forty-eighter who settled in Wisconsin and married a Swede, whose mother's father married an Englishwoman, whose son met a girl at college, whose mother was an Austrian and whose father was an Hungarian Jew and their son in the twentieth century right now is six feet tall and goes to a state college, plays football, and can't speak a word of any language except American."

> From the junior high text, Howard Wilder et al., *This Is America's Story*. (Boston: Houghton Mifflin Company, 1970), p. 550.

*   *   *   *   *

Furthermore, the relative improvement of the economic status of Negroes that began during World War II had not been sufficient. Automation hit the Negro workers with peculiar force, since many of them were unskilled and had received inferior schooling. Despite court decisions and federal policies, Negroes were becoming increasingly segregated in the North, often more so than in the South. As they moved into new city districts the whites moved out . . . .

The riots of the 1960's showed that mere attainment of paper rights was not enough to assuage the blacks' sense of rejection and injustice . . . . Every outbreak tended to harden white prejudice. The latter aspect was the most difficult of all. As President Johnson's commission to investigate the disorder reported: "What white

Many immigrants settled in crowded ethnic communities of New York's lower East Side. Courtesy The Bettmann Archive, Inc.

Americans have never fully understood—but what the Negro can never forget—is that white society is deeply implicated in the ghetto. White institutions created it, white institutions maintain it, and white society condones it."

> From the senior high text, Henry Bragdon and Samuel McCutchen, *History of a Free People* (New York: Macmillan Company, 1969), pp. 771-772.

GUIDELINES FOR EXAMINING TREATMENT OF
TOPIC OF IMMIGRATION IN AMERICAN HISTORY TEXTBOOKS

Does the text picture immigration as an ongoing process from colonial times to the present, or does it confine it to waves of foreigners coming to a settled America?

Are the newcomers brushed in tones of "tired" or "poor," the outcasts of their native lands, or does the text show a spectrum of types?

Does the text make a point to show inferiority of "new immigration" (after 1890) to that of the "old," or does it present two groups much alike in their reasons for coming, the skills and resources they brought with them, and their ability to adapt to American conditions?

Does the text make it appear that the problems America incurred by opening its door outweighed the advantages of labor, skills, talent, and intellect supplied by immigrants, or vice versa?

Does the text view immigration solely in terms of problems caused by immigrants, or does it look sympathetically at their conditions and the difficulties they had as well?

Does the text imply that American ethnic diversity came with the new immigration or does it point out that religious and other ethnic differences existed in this country from its founding and does it provide examples of ethnic cooperation and conflict?

Does the text stress that internal factors in America (great need for cheap labor, for example) as well as European conditions were responsible for immigration, or does it gloss over the former?

Are new immigrants scolded for living in "Little Italys," ethnic ghettos, while no mention is made that all immigrants have attempted to recreate Old World societies?

Are white ethnic groups, their children, and grandchildren credited with rapid assimilation so much so that ethnic groups seem to disappear altogether, or does the text mention the survival of national origins groups?

Are the social consequences of discrimination ignored, or are they illustrated by the successive uses of slums by immigrants and minorities, and by the economic handicaps imposed in the employment of immigrants in backbreaking, dangerous, and undesirable occupations?

Are subjects such as labor movements, city growth, political activity, denominational organization, and educational reform discussed without reference to the ethnic identity of the workers, citizens, voters, parishioners, and children?

Americans – Who Are They?

What you have just read about immigrant and ethnic groups in America is typical of the subject's treatment in most school history textbooks. These texts suggest that everything important in the American past has been said and done by white, English-speaking, old-stock Americans. Until very recently blacks, Indians, Mexican Americans, and the immigrants who arrived after America's earlier settlement have been the invisible people of American history— presented as faceless mobs, crowds, and "teeming refuse" as the poem on the Statue of Liberty puts it. Post-Revolutionary-period immigrants receive only token treatment in a few pages, sandwiched between the railroad and canal building era (1820–1850) and the Gilded Age (1870–1900).

What little is said tends to favor the northeastern Europeans known as the "old immigrants." Their adjustment is pictured as rapid, due to their dispersion to all areas of the country and their easier adaptation to native-American customs. In contrast, the "new immigrants" who came after 1890 from southern and eastern Europe are frequently treated unsympathetically. Writers paint them in darker colors and stress that they competed unfairly with the old-stock Americans, to take away their jobs and lower wages. Rather than conveniently dispersing to bright, wholesome farms as the "old immigrants" had done, this later newcomer willfully huddles in crowded, unsanitary, gloomy ghettos, to perpetuate foreign, and by implication un-American, customs. Yet, when viewed optimistically, the descendants of this alien mass will turn their backs on their own past and join the American mainstream.

To be an American, these textbook authors imply, is to conform to a presumed American pattern. As Israel Zangwell, the English dramatist, put it in his play *The Melting Pot,* "America is God's

Crowded apartment of turn-of-the-century immigrant family. Courtesy The Bettmann Archive, Inc.

crucible, the Great Melting Pot where all races of Europe are merging and reforming . . . German and Frenchman, Irishmen and Englishmen, Jews and Russians—into the Crucible with you all! God is making an American.''

The textbook picture of the immigrant credits the newcomers with great social and economic upward mobility. These immigrants, and particularly their descendants, become completely Americanized, indistinguishable from old-stock natives; they leave the ghetto and become affluent. When the texts present subgroups in American society, a white homogeneous group confronts a black group left out of the American mainstream.

The purpose of this study is to present a different view of American history and American society. The lessons and materials attempt to show the persistence and importance of ethnicity in American life. Ethnicity is best defined as group consciousness based on a sense of common origin. This group feeling can be centered around racial, religious, and national origins. While there is a collective identity with apparent common values and lifestyle we call ''American,'' Americans also belong to ethnic subgroups which influence their social, economic, and political life.

The homogenized picture of America where people are viewed primarily as individuals—and race, religion, and national origin do not really matter—is erroneous. Our textbooks have finally recognized that the attempt to alter black Americans in the melting pot has been a failure. What the texts often do not acknowledge is that we are a nation of many backgrounds and cultures. They fail to ask the question: How well have other groups who immigrated here adjusted and been absorbed by the old-stock native Americans?

In 1967 President Lyndon Johnson appointed a Commission on Civil Disorders to investigate the riots that were occurring in America's cities. The commission's conclusion was: "Our nation is moving toward two societies, one black, one white—separate and unequal." This study maintains that that statement is too simplistic—there are a number of subsocieties.

The first part of this study attempts to show that many large cities, with the city of Philadelphia taken as an example, contain ethnic neighborhoods—sections where there are high concentrations of people having a similar ethnic background. The similarities and differences in lifestyle are apparent. The second part explores organizations and institutions that serve various ethnic groups. The third part of this study dwells on the relationship of ethnicity to politics to suggest how ethnicity makes a difference in party preference, voting habits, and political issues.

Growing out of these three areas—ethnicity as expressed in neighborhoods, organizations, and politics—are a number of public issues. Often social science texts ignore or present simplistically the ethnic components of these issues (considering them only as results of the biases of ethnics). This study seeks to identify the ethnic component and present it in a more rounded and fair-minded way.

Data defines blacks as an ethnic group because of their unique history in America and examines this group along with others. Their experience has been more severe than that of white immigrant groups because of feelings passed on from years of slavery and because prejudice against color is deep-seated, and blacks could not disguise their identities. However, the assumption is made in this study that the black-white situation today can best be understood from a multiethnic perspective.

This program concludes with questionnaires that ask you to reexamine opinions held at the beginning of the study. Negative evidence is introduced, an essay which challenges the ethnic explanation of behavior. This will afford you a chance to summarize what you have learned and test it against another interpretation.

In ethnic neighborhoods the homes of residents are clustered about the schools, churches, and other institutions that are a part of their lives. Courtesy Herbert K. Barnett / University of Pittsburgh.

Ethnicity as Expressed in Neighborhoods

In the decade before World War I immigration averaged a million persons a year, and by 1914 over two-thirds of these immigrants were coming from southern and eastern Europe. Like the immigrants who preceded them, these newcomers tended to live near each other, forming communities of people having the same national origin. Unlike earlier immigrants who settled in rural areas, the later immigrants settled in cities where they found jobs in America's factories hungry for unskilled workers. Every great metropolis had a "Little Italy," a "Little Poland," a "Little Greece," or "Little Jerusalem," and so on. Have these immigrant ghettos completely disappeared with time and the succeeding generations of American-born children, or can we find ethnic neighborhoods remaining today? The data of this part of our study seeks to answer this question.

If there are identifiable ethnic groups, how do we locate them? That is the problem tackled in Topics 8 and 9. The first experience has you map an area and the second suggests photographs of ethnic clues. If ethnic groups are clustering in neighborhoods as Theme Three states, they can be found.

Very often when the subject of ethnic concentration is brought up, the reason offered is discrimination, specific acts of rejection against a group, which explains separation. The assumption is made that were discrimination to end, America's diverse peoples would integrate with each other as salt in soup. Are there voluntary as well as involuntary reasons for residential concentration? The answer to this question preoccupies Theme Four.

The immigrant ghetto has been pictured as a dreary, unhealthy place where unpleasant experiences happened to inhabitants. Is this the whole story? Life among people sharing a culture had some positive aspects, and an examination of these takes place as Topic 12 looks at the past, while Topic 13 observes the descendants of immigrants and blacks in working-class ethnic neighborhoods.

Theme Six introduces three important public issues that grow out of ethnic-group neighborhood concentration. In the name of progress cities seek to build superhighways, expand factories, and permit colleges to add facilities, or seek to tear down "unsightly" structures and replace with all sorts of buildings, housing projects, or shiny, new office and business centers. Most often this progress is at the expense of residents of working-class neighborhoods where ethnic-group concentration is highest. What should be done? Topics 14 and 16 present the problems for you to think over.

An American institution has grown up that is known as the neighborhood school. People desiring to live near one another also like to have their children associate with one another at school. The values and ways of doing things are familiar. Busing for integration, seeking racial balance in black-white terms raises many fears. Unsure of what will happen, nonblack parents (in the material presented in this case, Chinese) see the court order as a threat to their community. Topic 15 introduces this thorny issue. There are no easy answers, but these are persisting questions that all of us must be informed about and for which the opportunity will come to make some hard decisions.

Ethnic Groups in Neighborhoods

The family is a very important part of ethnic neighborhoods, for the members help one another know who they are and provide connections with neighborhood residents and institutions.

TOPIC 8

Who Lives in Our Community?

Most schools have district boundary lines to indicate the area from inside of which residents are permitted to send students to attend classes. Your teacher will tell you the boundaries of the area from which your school draws its population. This is the neighborhood school principle; students attend the school nearest their homes. However, some classmates come from miles away. They are granted this privilege for good reasons.

The data for this learning experience will be gathered by members of the class. You will need detailed street maps of the city.

Directions for mapping the distribution of ethnic groups in your community:

1. Outline boundaries of the neighborhood that feeds your school.
2. If you live outside the school boundaries, use your home as a focal point and outline two blocks on all sides.
3. For purposes of this study ethnic groups are viewed as including all groups defined by race, religion, language, national or regional origin. For example, blacks, Ukrainians, Poles, Germans, Italians, Armenians, Cubans, Jews, and Southern Protestant whites are ethnic groups.
4. Decide on a code or legend of color for various ethnic groups. If there are more than three in an area, label and code as "mixed."
5. Divide yourselves into teams of four, trying to choose partners from those who live near you.
6. Develop a grid system and superimpose it on the area of city map outlined by your school boundaries. Each team will commit itself to a cell on the grid.
7. Each team will interview four members of the community within its cell: residents, storekeepers, political party committeemen, and other politicians.

40

8. Each field researcher on the team should be prepared to introduce himself or herself, explaining the purpose of the study, that it is a class project to make a map of locations of ethnic groups in the neighborhood. You may want your teacher to ditto copies of a letter of introduction.
9. Ask the following questions:
    1) Do you know whether most of the people living in this neighborhood—at least half the residents—are members of one ethnic group? (Give examples of ethnic groups.)
    2) If not, are there two or three ethnic groups that together make up at least half the population of the neighborhood? If so, which groups?
    3) If not, are there three ethnic groups in the neighborhood? If so, which groups?
    4) If there are more than three, have respondant list as many as possible. (A mixed area)
    5) For any of the above name specific streets and blocks where the ethnic groups mentioned are living.
10. Have information coded, plot on maps by drawing lines around areas occupied by ethnic groups and color in.
11. Have one map in the classroom as a base map and hold one member of each team responsible for giving data to a class member designated as the cartographer, who will plot a line for each ethnic group on base map that connects places on the map where members of that group live.

How Can We Recognize
an Ethnic Neighborhood?

In the previous topic you may have found evidence of ethnic group concentration by interviewing residents and mapping out areas. This lesson suggests visual indicators of ethnic group concentration. The photos that follow contain a number of clues or indicators which reveal the presence of an ethnic group in a section. The presence of one ethnic group or another helps to shape some of the features of a neighborhood.

As you examine these photos, try to identify the various indicators and features of these neighborhoods. Be ready to compare and contrast these features. Classify these features into categories which can be used to determine whether or not there is a concentration of racial, religious, or national origins group in an area of a city.

Ethnic Neighborhoods Result from Voluntary and Involuntary Factors

Many ethnics, such as the Chinese who settled in New York's Chinatown, grouped together to preserve their identity and culture. Courtesy Wide World Photos.

How Come You Live Here?

Many of America's large cities contain a number of different ethnic neighborhoods, each of which has certain distinguishing features. These features we have called ethnic indicators, since they serve as clues to the background of the residents in the neighborhood. In viewing the photos you noticed these clues: ethnic churches, religious stores, fraternal organizations, cemeteries, names of merchants and professional people, stores specializing in ethnic foods, foreign language newspapers, and so on. Why do people live in ethnic neighborhoods? Your parents will explain the reasons why they live where they do. You will read transcripts of recorded interviews of residents who live in the areas you viewed in the photos. *Do the reasons your parents gave hold true for these residents? Why do people of the same ethnic background wish to live near one another?*

TRANSCRIPTIONS OF TAPED INTERVIEWS*

Charles Miarchi, a successful Italian-American lawyer and now judge of the Municipal Court of Philadelphia, has both his residence and law office near Broad and Federal streets in South Philadelphia:

I think we developed an affinity for the community, growing up in it and getting to know the people, going to school here in the community—Southern High and later Temple Law—and then estab-

*Taped by Philip Rosen, instructor in history, Northeast High School, Philadelphia, Summer 1970.

lishing the practice of law here. We seem to identify with the community by being involved in politics, scouting, and other areas of social-communal activities. I really feel like I have roots here.

In the area around 1600 South, near Broad, you have homes that have been completely rebuilt by the children of the original owners. The property values have increased from what was originally $5,000 or $6,000 some years ago to a point where these homes are now in the category of $35,000 to $50,000. The improvements have included air conditioning, gas heat, new fronts of stone, new kitchens, complete modernization from attic to cellar, often done with the labor of the owner and his family's hands.

My wife, five children, and myself live in this house where I was born. In many, many of the homes the parents of the children live with them. It is common in this community for the children to take care of their parents as they age. There is a cross section of occupations within these few blocks. There are several doctors, some lawyers, Ph.D.'s in physics, city employees, housewives, people who work for the Navy Yard, for the Budd Company. Of the skilled occupations all of the building trades would predominate. We have a good cross section of the tailoring industry, too, where both men and women have worked in the tailor shops for many, many years.

Mrs. George T. Dukes, Afro-American, a Cornell graduate in social work, mother of three, and a community worker, resides in Southwest Central Philadelphia, sometimes called South Street:

I was born in South Philadelphia in this community and lived here for a number of years until my family moved away. My husband was also born and raised in this community and lived here until we were married. We decided to move back into South Philadelphia in July 1959 for two reasons: we liked the geographical area. I can look out my back and see William Penn at night, and I can take a short walk and be right on Walnut and Chestnut streets in center city. The other reason is that my husband and I read a study by a Mr. Levin urging white suburbanites to move back into the inner city. We felt that if we came back into the community we could work with the community organizations so that when whites came in, Negroes would not be totally removed.

My husband, Mr. George Dukes, works at the Children's Hospital a few blocks from here. He is running for State Senator because he feels that the man currently in that office doesn't live in this neighborhood and is indifferent to the problems of the neighborhood. I am the president of my block association, which I helped to organize, and am on the board of the Southwest Central City Citizen's Council, the Center City Y.W.C.A., second vice-president of the district board of the Health and Welfare Council, chairman of the Southern Area Health and Welfare Council, and chairman of the League of Women Voters Voters' Education Program.

It is much easier for a Caucasion to move and live where he chooses than it is for a black person. This neighborhood has people from all socioeconomic backgrounds. The deputy superintendent of Philadelphia Schools, Robert Poindexter, lives near us. Yet some people here live on welfare.

These homes are large and well-made. Real-estate dealers know that and wish to fix them up for whites who want to live in center city—those that can afford $70,000.

Michael O'Regan, an immigrant from Ireland, a coal dealer, has resided in Schuylkill for over forty-five years:

Being originally from Boston and having some history in Boston, I appreciate the history of Schuylkill which goes right back to the American Revolution. I had some friends in Schuylkill when I came to Philadelphia in 1928 from New York. I had a job with the government during World War I, and in 1928 I was able to get a job at the Mint here in Philadelphia. Every nationality, I guess, goes where the majority of their people are. My friends brought me to Schuylkill, and I married a girl who is a native of Schuylkill.

Robert Tomar, a druggist, and his wife Jeannette, a school secretary, have resided for many years in the Oxford Circle section, an area with a heavy Jewish population.

Mrs. Tomar:

We were both living in South Philadelphia when we were single. I lived at Third and Ritner, and my husband, Robert, lived at Fifth and Tasker, in that vicinity. When we married, we moved to an apartment in West Philadelphia which was convenient to the school my husband was attending. After our first child was born we sought to buy a house in another area, and after looking carefully, we decided to move to the Oxford Circle. We moved into the area primarily because we thought it was a predominantly Jewish section and we preferred living in a more Jewish neighborhood.

Mr. Tomar:

In going to and from institutions in South Philadelphia—the library and the Hebrew School outside my immediate neighborhood—we had to encroach upon Gentile neighborhoods where we met with animosity, beatings, and name-calling. To protect ourselves we had to travel in gangs—groups, actually, of four or five kids. The library was located at Fifth and Washington. To go there required the carrying of baseball bats and broomsticks because it was that rough. There was a factory at one time that was torn down, and the gangs used to lay in wait there and throw bricks and stones at us. There were incidents of J, for Jew, carvings on the body with a knife. I felt that by moving to a more Jewish neighborhood I might possibly avoid my children having to go through that torture, animosity, whatever you call it.

Mrs. Tomar:

When we were originally seeking a house to buy, my husband wanted to move to New Jersey. I fought this because it would mean more difficulty in seeing and talking to our parents, and this is one of the reasons we stayed in Philadelphia—to be close to our family. Also, because many of the areas in Jersey are not Jewish at all. I want to raise my children in a Jewish atmosphere.

How Did the Immigrant Ghetto Form?

You have identified the reasons why your parents moved into your neighborhood and you have heard reasons why residents of four different neighborhoods live where they do. Now you will read what historians have said about the forming of ethnic neighborhoods. Although not every immigrant group is represented in these selections, many of the reasons given for one group apply to all. Blacks are included as newcomers, for they were internal immigrants. Americans by birth for generations, most blacks resided initially in the South, migrating to the North only over the past sixty years. Like the ''new immigrants,'' they came from rural, agricultural regions where they suffered from second-class status.

Read each selection carefully and check the reasons offered by the historians against the list you compiled for moving into a neighborhood from the previous learning activity. These reasons may be categorized as *push factors* and *pull factors*. Push factors are unpleasant, negative reasons pushing a person away from certain areas. Pull factors are voluntary, self-imposed forces that draw a person toward a particular place. *As you read, categorize the reasons under these two headings. Read the statements about the formation of the black ghetto (Selection 1) first and then determine whether the same reasons apply for the other immigrant ghettos.*

Selection 1

Smarting from the effects of Jim Crow, living in fear of lynching, seeing their labor replaced by agricultural mechanization, and hearing of wonderful wages paid in war industries, the southern black moved north. Between 1910 and 1960 over 45 percent of the

Girls at play in the neighborhood of Hiram House, Cleveland, 1925. Courtesy Western Reserve Historical Society.

southern blacks migrated to mainly six states: California, Illinois, Michigan, New York, Ohio, and Pennsylvania.

The black migrants converged on the older sections of the central city because the lowest cost housing was there; friends and relatives were likely to be there; and these older neighborhoods often had good public transportation which would enable them to get to work quicker.

After a period of time black families attained higher incomes, higher living standards, and higher cultural refinements. However, these black families remained in all-black neighborhoods because they were effectively excluded from white residential areas. This exclusion has been accomplished through various discriminatory practices, some obvious and open, others subtle and hidden. These practices have included understandings among real estate dealers not to sell to black buyers, creation of a separate housing market for blacks, intimidation and threatening phone calls, cross-burning, and violence against the person and property of a new black neighbor.

Another form of discrimination is ''white flight''—withdrawal from or refusal to enter neighborhoods where large numbers of blacks are moving or already residing. Normal population turnover causes about 20 percent of the residents of average United States neighborhoods to move out every year because of income changes, job transfers, relocation because of aging or deaths. The refusal of whites to move into changing areas when vacancies occur there from normal turnover means that most vacancies are eventually occupied by blacks. This causes the shift toward heavy black occupancy. Once this happens, remaining whites seek to leave, for they have the belief once the blacks have entered, the neighborhood will be 100 percent black in a short time. As these whites move out, more blacks move in, and this belief becomes self-fulfilling.

> Adapted from *The Report of The National Advisory Commission on Civil Disorders* (New York: Bantam, 1968), pp. 237, 244–245.

Selection 2

The immigrants came to America for many reasons. Some came to escape tyranny or political persecution or to obtain religious freedom. Some came to escape wars, revolutions, foreign conquest, and the political changes that accompanied these. However, the economic motive dominated the minds of most immigrants. The Irish came to avoid starvation when their most stable crop, the potato, failed. Deep poverty, crop failure, and loss of land ownership drove the Italians to America for better living conditions. The Polish, Ruthenian, Slovak, Magyar, Croat, Serbian, and Slavic peasant sailed for America from central and eastern Europe because the whole farming economy was changing, and the peasant needed a job to support himself and his family. New laws in Russia excluded the Jews from areas and occupations in which they had earned a living for generations, so they set sail for the "Golden Land."

> By Philip Rosen, instructor in history, Northeast High School, Philadelphia, PA.

Selection 3

The great mass of late-nineteenth-century immigrants could not possibly have become farmers on arrival because they had so little money with them and starting a farm took some capital. The position of farm laborer did not attract them for a number of reasons: The job in Europe had a very low status; the language difficulty was more serious on the farm than in the factory; farm employment tended to be unsteady and the pay tended to be lower than in the factory. Most important, the Slavs (eastern and central Europeans) and the Italians had become accustomed in the old country to the intimate social contacts of village life. The loneliness of rural existence in America, where miles might separate neighbors, repelled them. Lastly, work on the farm dwindled as America's industrial revolution took hold in the latter part of the nineteenth century. Textbook writers who scold the "new immigrants" for not settling on the farmlands do not appraise the necessary adjustment the newcomers had to make. What else but concentration in the cities was to be expected from the newcomers at a time when even the children of native Americans were leaving the farms in droves for the cities? American industrial development attracted migrants from overseas; had they not known that work awaited them in the mines, mills, and factories, they would have not even crossed the Atlantic.

> Adapted from Maldwyn Jones, *American Immigration* (Chicago: University of Chicago Press, 1960), pp. 214–216.

Selection 4

Into a section of Philadelphia bounded by 2nd and 6th streets and extending from Lombard to Catherine streets came the first Jews who settled with the established residents. They chose this location for a number of reasons: South Street, its central thoroughfare, proved to be a good business district; second-hand goods of every variety could be purchased there; peddlers' supply houses were crammed with bargains that could be had on a week's credit; the street served as an emporia of rag shops and old clothing bazaars; and to the Jews of southern Russia the characteristics of the area brought back memories of the market places similar to the Odessa *tolchuk,* open air market, to which they were accustomed.

Other factors contributed to the choice of this neighborhood. Familiar signs with Hebrew characters which told where kosher food could be purchased satisfied the pious. The closeness of the area to the Federal, Washington, and Christian Street wharves where many got off the ships caused some to settle in the immediate neighborhood. Yet, the basic reason was the inexpensive living quarters that could be quickly obtained by those with little or no funds. This section had for years been the home of the vicious, the criminal, the transient, and the abandoned. Landlords could rent and sell to hardworking, clean-living immigrants.

The Poles and Italians settled near this area too. Each immigrant group concentrated in a low rental area where employment was readily available. Although separated from one another by customs and language, the Poles on the way to the factories passed the Italians on the way to the railroads and the Jews passed them both on the way to the clothing sweatshops. All shared in common the South Philadelphia location.

Adapted from Maxwell Whiteman,
"Jewish Pathfinders in South
Philadelphia," Philadelphia *Jewish Exponent* (April 24, 1964).

Selection 5

Prospective immigrants needed passage money and they often could not provide it themselves. Someone had to help them by sending over a prepaid ticket. Once arrived, the newcomer needed assistance in finding a place to live and a job; he needed the assistance of some knowledgeable person for this. Established immigrants, those who came before the newcomer, provided this help.

Much clothing manufacturing at the turn of century was done by immigrants in "sweatshops" such as this one. Courtesy Museum of the City of New York.

Often the benefactor was a father, uncle, cousin, or close friend, someone who spoke the same language of the newcomer, someone who came from his hometown. Among the Italians, Greeks, and Syrians certain enterprising established immigrants would lend passage money to prospective immigrants and later act as their foreman, real estate agent, legal advisor, and interpreter. These men called *padroni* (bosses) brought many people from a town in Europe to live in the same neighborhood of America. The immigrant lived with his fellow townsmen near his *padrone*.

Based on John S. MacDonald and Beatrice D. MacDonald, "Urbanization, Ethnic Groups, and Social Segmentation," *Social Research* 29 (1962): 443–444.

Selection 6

The Italian is by nature sociable. However, his clustering in the South Philadelphia quarter is not only due to his fondness for socializing and lack of means to enter the life of this country but also because he is sensitive to ridicule. Last to arrive among the waves of immigrants and, therefore, the least Americanized, he is the least understood by native-born Americans.

To avoid ridicule and for an active social life the Italian lives in Philadelphia with his *paesano,* fellow townsman from Italy. In this country *paesani* worship the same saints, speak the same dialect, intermarry, and belong to the same fraternal organizations. It used to be a familiar sight to anyone with some acquaintance with the Italians in this country to find one side or end of a city block populated by those from one small district in Italy, while on the opposite end dwelled those from another locality.

> Adapted from Sister M. Agnes Gertrude, "Italian Immigration into Philadelphia," *Records of the American Catholic Historical Society of Philadelphia,* September, 1947, pp. 189–190.

Selection 7

The less wealthy natives, the Anglo-Saxons, although by no means poor—they were small store owners, middle managers, clerical workers and professionals—were anxious to make the most of their incomes and wished, above all, to preserve their status. To them the influx of foreign-born people with low-paying jobs and homes jammed with more than one family and boarders represented a downgrading of the neighborhood. The proper identification— identification with good schools, neighborhood, churches, and societies—could open valuable opportunities for themselves and their children.

These people could not remain where they were when threatened by low-status newcomers. As the immigrants moved in, the Protestant churches found their Sunday school pupils, church service attendance, and membership dwindling so that the cost for those who remained mounted. The old shops lost their customers, while the newcomers attended shops where the storekeepers spoke

Giving out books to children in an ethnic neighborhood of earlier Cleveland. Courtesy Western Reserve Historical Society.

the language of the old country and where the goods and ways of selling were familiar. The public schools changed in character. Those who stayed felt engulfed in a new ethnic community. It became essential to move; the wisest thing to do at the sight of change was to abandon the neighborhood to the newcomer.

Adapted from Oscar Handlin, *The Newcomers* (Garden City, New Jersey: Anchor Books, 1962 edition), pp. 30–31.

Selection 8

As the American generation grew up, the immigrant parents thought of moving. The ghetto was no place to marry off a daughter. They looked for space and fresh air, and the sight of a bit of green. At first they moved to adjacent areas; when they were filled, they moved further out, the trolley lines and subways taking them beyond the intermediate settlements of other ethnic groups. The immigrant parents did not flee the ghetto. Far from it; they rather sought a superior place to which they could take the ghetto with them.

From Oscar Handlin, *Adventure in Freedom* (New York: McGraw-Hill, 1954), p. 104.

Selection 9

Isolation in ethnic neighborhoods of South Philadelphia provided a shelter for the newcomer, a place where he returned at night from work to learn the American city culture while living among his fellow beginners with whom he shared a common experience, language, and church. Similarly, the active street life provided excitement, companionship, and recreation for the more Americanized who remained in the district—the second generation, the sons of the immigrants, and those who could not afford to move into the lower middle-class districts of the west and northwest.

South Philadelphia, a district of 358,000 inhabitants in 1930, did not function as one giant neighborhood. Rather it was an area characterized by many neighborhoods, each one a place where neighbors depended upon one another, where relatives, ethnic churches, and ethnic societies abounded. Poor people and working-class people could make a stable family life in this section of Philadelphia. Few people moved out of the area. This stability, family ties of mutual demands, loyalties of friends, of the gang, of the street and the saloon, all were necessities to help bolster the families and individuals of South Philadelphia against the successive crises of poverty. For many families unemployment each year was a fact of life. Heavy proportions of the district's workers labored in low-skill, low-paid marine and transport jobs, in the low-pay and seasonal garment industry, in the regular work of the building trades and the unrewarding service jobs. At home, after work, the South Philadelphia worker found comfort, aid, and a satisfactory sense of identity in his neighborhood.

Adapted from Sam Bass Warner, *The Private City* (Philadelphia: University of Pennsylvania, 1968), pp. 185–186.

THEME FIVE

Ethnic Group Life-Styles in Neighborhoods

Ethnic peoples expressing their religious identity in celebrating the festival of St. Januarius in Little Italy, New York City. Courtesy Wide World Photos.

59

What Was a Ghetto Like?

Huddled into a small, densely populated section of the city characterized by shanties, tenements, bandbox and ramshackle houses dwelt the newcomers. They endured the damp cold of winter and the stifling, dead heat of summer. Rats and other vermin fed on garbage and filth that lay in inaccessible alleys, in open sewers, in the outhouses that dotted the yards. The ghetto could be identified from blocks away by the stench of rotting things.

Shelter meant one or two rooms that served for bedrooms, kitchen, and living room. Little privacy came from the sheets that divided parts of the rooms. Many infants died at birth or soon after, as death in the form of disease stalked the neighborhoods. Tuberculosis scored the highest among the killers of young and old alike. Women lost their bloom of youth early, while a man counted himself lucky if he celebrated his forty-fifth birthday. Poverty, aggravated by recurring periods of unemployment, plagued these newcomers who had to accept the most undesirable, low-paying, menial jobs. Children, tender in age, who could have been in school or on the playground, trudged to work each morning along with the adults.

Such is the picture of the immigrant ghetto painted by many social and urban historians. But does the above characterization tell the whole story? You read in the previous lesson how newcomers formed a society that gave him solace against the viciousness of the environment. Immigrants kept coming from overseas; blacks kept moving up from the South. Although their possessions counted little more than what they wore on their backs, much of what these people brought with them remained hidden in their memories—their culture. *As you read, jot down how this "cultural baggage" expressed itself in the ghetto.*

Robert Sebastian grew up in South Philadelphia and graduated from South Philadelphia High School and the Law School of the University of Pennsylvania. He became a well-known and respected practicing attorney in the city. He is currently the assistant grand master of the Sons of Italy Lodge and a member of the nine-man Philadelphia Board of Education.

Robert Sebastian Remembers Little Italy

The hub of the so-called "Little Italy" was the old Palumbo restaurant and hotel located at Catherine and Darien streets. The Palumbo family aided new immigrants as they came off the boat by providing temporary lodging for them at the hotel and directing them to jobs in the city. Around 7th and Christian there was an Italian bookstore known as Bisciotti that sold the latest publications in the Italian language—books, magazines, and newspapers. Right close by were several stores that sold records. The Victrola, the record player of that day, had become a popular article for the home; it got a tremendous impetus with the coming into prominence of great singers like Caruso, the tenor; Tetracini, the soprano; and Tita Ruffo, the baritone. These Italian artists were making tremendous names for themselves all over the world, and, of course, the Italian immigrants in Little Italy bought their records avidly.

Also in that area, somewhere around 8th and Christian, was the Italian theater that specialized in vaudeville and produced shows with dialog and songs in Italian.

Around 9th Street, starting as far south as Wharton and going up as far north as Fitzwater, was the 9th Street Market. That's where the pushcarts and the open-air stands were that sold vegetables, fruit, and fish, where the families residing in Little Italy and elsewhere did their shopping. Here they could buy food and goods similar to what was sold in the old country. In this area also there was a number of small stores that constituted the tradesmen's group.

Adapted from a taped interview with Mr. Sebastian by Philip Rosen, instructor in history, Northeast High School, Philadelphia, Summer 1970.

Open-market shopping in an ethnic neighborhood. What kinds of products do you think would be sold here that are not found elsewhere?

These included barbershops, shoemending shops, tailor shops, and piano repair-and-tuning shops. Around 1915 the pianola became very important, a great status symbol in Little Italy. I remember that when my family bought a pianola, we started to receive many friends in our house to see and play on the pianola.

There were a number of stores that sold musical instruments because many of the Italian immigrants earned their living or picked up an extra dollar in the field of music. Musicians played at funerals, for there would always be a band accompanying the hearse from the house to the church and back again. A common, almost daily, occurrence was the funeral with a band walking behind. Many a morning I was awakened by the thud of the drums and the brassy instruments. Musicians were popular at weddings, christenings, baptisms, and confirmations as well as on saints' days.

As children we went to school and made friends with our classmates. There was no shortage of schools either public or private. The Italians sent their children to both. I went to public school. The achievement was to get past the eighth grade. The elementary diploma would rank very much with a high-school diploma today. I went to a high school [South Philadelphia] that was about 95 percent Jewish, yet I always felt a closeness with my fellow students. I learned some Yiddish from them, and they learned some Italian from me. There would be some bantering back and forth as far as our religious and ethnic differences, but there was always warmth and friendship.

To the east and to the south of the Italian colony were Jews. Also in the areas where you did your shopping—for clothing and hardware—there would be Jewish shopkeepers. I remember when we lived at Juniper and Federal, my mother would go about Easter time and buy our suits and shoes and other Easter finery at the shops on Federal Street. The Jewish shopkeepers were numerous between 16th and 18th streets. It was always a game you know. My mother always prided herself on being able to buy things cheaper than they were worth, and in her broken English she would always engage in some very shrewd negotiating. It was the rule of the game that when you went to the shop, you were going to be charged more than you were willing to pay. It was something like the bargaining that goes on in the Arab nations, where it is a personal affront to both the buyer and seller to pay the price originally asked.

The streets served as the place where we children used to play most of our games. There wasn't much equipment. We used to strike a little piece of wood with a larger one to give it propulsion. We played such games as "Buck, Buck—Number One is Coming" and a number of others that may have had their origin in Italy. Games took place in the school yard, too, and where I lived at 13th and Federal. Passyunk Square, which extended from 13th to 12th and from Wharton to Reed, was a beautiful park. It had apple-blossom trees and other beautiful blooming trees under which neighbors would sit and talk. We began encroaching on the park in a corner where we would play baseball and other games. The older folks would rather see us there than on the streets.

Of course, at that time there was no radio or television. If you were well-off you could get to the movies once every two weeks. It was always a treat to go to the Saturday afternoon show; often there were special prizes for children.

Sunday was church day, and many activities centered about the church. I remember the feast days—each church had its own feast day. I lived in St. Rita's parish, and the month of May belonged to her, so that special services occurred at the church the entire month. On the feast day you could buy hot dogs; you also could get soft drinks and wine at outdoor stands. A band would play old songs from Italy as the statues of the saints were led out of the church and around the neighborhood, and money donated to the church would be pinned on the statues. At night we kids were thrilled by the display of fireworks that ended the celebration of the day.

Another custom carried over from the south Italian villages was the celebration of a name day. A birthday goes by like any other day, but your name day, which was after a saint, was an important day; you would receive cards and a feast. St. Anthony was important in my family because that was my father's first name, and we had as big a feast as we would at Christmas. Much wine was served. Wine, however, flowed at every meal, but generally the consumption was very restrained. Everybody I knew drank it, the children, too, all in moderation. A drunkard would be the neighborhood character; he would sing operatic melodies in the middle of the night and be arrested. The American press would spotlight this to consider the Italians a bunch of drunkards, but this was far from the truth.

Everything now is one great wasteland of popular trademarks, in food, in drugs, and in clothing. There is no room left for all the very attractive, individual variations of those earlier days. When we were kids my mother used to buy special Italian soap in a drug store at 9th and Carpenter owned by an Uncle of mine. There were different perfumed soaps from Italy. At Christmas time we would get different chocolates from Italy, and we would look forward to these things because they were unique and different. Today people buy the soap where they can get the best bargain from the supermarket. The flavor of the Italian-American culture is disappearing.

Marian Anderson is an outstanding black singer born and raised in Philadelphia. A famous woman today, sought after for the most prestigious singing roles, Miss Anderson recalls the past, the neighborhood, her parents, and those people who helped her achieve fame.

Growing Up in South Philadelphia

I was born on Webster Street in South Philadelphia in a room my parents had rented when they were married . . . .

As the family increased, so did the need for larger quarters, and we moved again . . . . This house did not have a real bathroom, but Mother was undaunted. We were lathered and rinsed at least once a day, and on Saturday a huge wooden tub was set in the center of the kitchen floor. After sufficiently warm water was poured in, we were lifted inside. Mother would kneel and give us a good scrubbing with Ivory soap. Then we were put to bed . . . .

Our big outing each year was a trip to the Barnum and Bailey Circus. To us it was like a great journey away from home. We prepared for the day long in advance; it was the next biggest day to Christmas. Father would buy us something new to wear. A basket or two was prepared, and off we went, taking a trolley car for what seemed like an endless ride. We had wonderful lunches and afternoon snacks. Our eyes were big with delight, trying to follow all the acts going on at the same time under the big tent. Then we trudged wearily to the trolley and took the long ride home. By then we were so tired that our parents must have had a bad time getting us ready for bed . . . .

. . . employed by day at the Reading Terminal Market, in the refrigerator room, . . . Father took pride in his chores at the Union Baptist Church. He was a special officer there, and among other things had charge of the ushers. He received no pay for his service; it was something that a person did out of love for his religion and duty to his church. He loved this job and never missed a Sunday at church.

Even before I was six I was taken along to church every Sunday, partly, I suppose, to alleviate my mother's burden of taking care of three children. I would take part in the Sunday School and then sit through the main service. After my sixth birthday I was enrolled in the junior choir of the church . . . .

Adapted from Marian Anderson, *My Lord What a Morning* (New York: Viking Press, 1956), pp. 4–56.

Mother saw to it that we were in earnest about our schooling. She has always had a way of saying things that I feel are things to live by. About school tasks at home, she said, "If it takes you half an hour to do your lessons and it takes someone else fifteen minutes, take the half-hour and do them right." . . .

. . . Father died in our home on Colorado Street. . . . Even if I had been old enough to work, I know now, Mother would have discouraged it. She believed in education. When I completed grammar school I went on to high school. The first I attended was William Penn High School, where I started with the idea of taking a commercial course. I knew deep in my heart by this time that what I wanted most was to study music, but I also knew that I had to prepare myself to get a job as soon as possible—both to help Mother and to have some money for music studies. . . .

. . . My heart was not in these [commercial] studies, and I was happiest when we had our music period once a week. . . .I once sang some solos at an assembly attended by visitors. Afterward I was summoned to the principal's office. . . . When I entered the room [a visitor] turned to the principal and said, "I don't understand why this girl is taking shorthand and typing. She should have a straight college preparatory course and do as much as possible in music." . . .

. . . we had a big concert at the Union Baptist Church once a year. . . . The person most often engaged for the gala concert was Roland Hayes, the distinguished tenor. . . . He came to visit Grandmother, and he told her that I should start professional studies. . . . Grandmother told Mr. Hayes that we had no money to pay for lessons. . . .

Then the congregation, led by Reverend Parks, decided to do something for me. The pastor arranged to take up a collection at a service. I remember his words: "We want to do something for our Marian." . . . The money was turned over to Mother, and she was told that it was for anything I needed. . . . What I needed was shoes. . . . I also needed a dress for special occasions. . . .

I sensed the need for a formal musical education when I was in my teens and was beginning to make my first modest tours. I decided, in fact, to see if I could not go to a music school. . . . I went there one day when enrollments were beginning, and I took my

Marian Anderson, at the end of a long and successful career, waves farewell after a Carnegie Hall concert in 1965. Courtesy Wide World Photos.

place in line. There was a young girl behind a cage who answered questions and gave out application blanks to be filled out. When my turn came she looked past me and called on the person standing behind me. This went on until there was no one else in line. Then she spoke to me, and her voice was not friendly. "What do *you* want?"

I tried to ignore her manner and replied that I had come to make inquiries regarding an application for entry to the school.

She looked at me coldly and said, "We don't take colored." . . .

It must be remembered that we grew up in a mixed neighborhood. White and Negro lived side by side and shared joys and sorrows. At school and on the street we encountered all kinds of children. Did we live in a poor neighborhood? "Poor" is relative. Some people owned their homes in that street and considered themselves well off. We had enough to eat and we dressed decently. We were not so poor that we had nothing, and our neighbors were in the same situation.

There were times when we heard our relatives and friends talking, and we knew we might come in contact with this, that, or the other thing. In some stores we might have to stand around longer than other people until we were waited on. There were times when we stood on a street corner, waiting for a trolley car, and the motorman would pass us by. There were places in town where all people could go, and there were others where some of us could not go. There were girls we played with and others we didn't. There were parties we went to, and some we didn't. We were interested in neither the places nor the people who did not want us . . . .

[In need of professional training, Miss Anderson appeared before Mr. Boghetti, a friend of the principal of her school, then South Philadelphia High.]

My song was "Deep River." I did not look at Mr. Boghetti as I sang, and my eyes were averted from him when I had finished. He came to the point quickly. "I will make room for you right away," he said firmly, "and I will need only two years with you. After that, you will be able to go anywhere and sing for anybody." . . .

. . . This man had an odd magnetic quality. He would sit in one of the front rows and fix his eyes squarely on yours when you were singing. Somehow he helped you sing better than you thought you could. I noticed that he had this effect on me when I sang in regular halls in Philadelphia. He was sure to be in a seat up front where I could see him. I knew he was watching me, and I just had to do what he expected of me.

There came a time when the money provided for the lessons by my friends and neighbors was exhausted, but Mr. Boghetti did not put me out of his studio . . . . Indeed, he carried me without payment of any kind for more than a year. During this period he went so far as to say that I need not pay and that he was wiping out the arrears. I am certain that he meant it, but in time I was fortunate to be able to repay him in full.

Once Detroit was rich with a mosaic of ethnic neighborhoods which
    have become dispersed or partially shattered by the impact of

urban life. Now urbanologists—in contradiction of the old Melting Pot theory—say such groups are one measure of the vitality of a city. In the first of four articles, Staff Writer Marco Trbovich examines the changes in the fortunes of three Roman Catholic parishes in what was once "Poletown," Detroit's oldest Polish-American community.

Life in Detroit's Poletown

Joe Walkowski's body slumped to the scarlet carpet of St. Josaphat church with a muffled thud. Father Francis Dolot stopped the mass. Joe's wife rushed to his side. Parishioners crowded around. It was too late. His heart had failed. Joe was dead.

Years later Father Dolot would say there was something almost poetic about Joe's death: something like a blessing that he should die in the church to which he had given so much of his life.

For Joe Walkowski was Polish. Baptized in St. Josaphat; reared on St. Antoine across the street from that same Polish church in the days when people were known by their parish, not by the name of their neighborhood. He went to grade school there; was confirmed there; married and later celebrated his silver anniversary there. And finally, Joe Walkowski was buried from St. Josaphat.

Thousands of Polish-American Detroiters grew up like Joe in Poletown; in the wood-frame parishes around three churches on the east side.

The churches still stand, rising above vacant lots scruffy with weeds, above tattered wood houses, and gutted, black-eyed shops: St. Albertus, at Canfield and St. Aubin; Sweetest Heart of Mary, at Canfield and Russell; St. Josaphat, at Canfield and Chrysler—a configuration, one old timer said, that once made Canfield "the Polish Woodward."

"A monument to the Poles," an ardent young advocate of Polish culture called these churches.

Excerpted from Marco Trbovich, "Ethnic Detroit, Polish Life," *Detroit Free Press*, March 25, 1973.

But though they still stand, the Poles who attended them have, for the most part, moved—virtually en masse. And unlike Joe Walkowski, who returned from his new home in northeast Detroit to the parish of his youth, they have made their exodus complete by joining new churches in Detroit, Warren and other suburbs.

They were replaced in Poletown by blacks; and they in turn by the bulldozer, leaving only sprigs of concrete foundations jutting from the ground like broken teeth—monuments to nothing so much as the cycle of urban decay that has laid waste to ethnic enclaves throughout Detroit.

The three parishes now have memberships of some 300 families each in churches that once were packed with more than a thousand parishioners at every Sunday mass.

Life in Poletown in those earlier days was culturally rich. The neighborhood was self-contained and self-sufficient. Father Boguslaus Poznanski, pastor of Sweetest Heart of Mary, described "a cluster of businessmen: The doctors, the dentists; they came from here and they took care of the people here."

Butcher shops and bakeries were sprinkled throughout the near east side, and always near the churches were funeral homes run by Poles: Chrzanowski's on Russell; Wujek's around the corner on Canfield. Down the street was Zynda's brewery, to supply life's livelier moments. And in a nearby office, the Polish Daily Record chronicled Poletown's life.

The streets were vibrant with life in an area that is now virtually deserted night and day.

"I still miss it," said Julia Pisarski, who moved to Sterling Heights but maintains her membership at St. Albertus.

"Everything was Polish in that neighborhood. When I was a kid I remember the day after Easter the friends would come to our house and switch the girls (with twigs). My father's day was St. John's day. And feast days, name days, they were more important than a birthday." . . .

She remembered, too, that all the women in the neighborhood would go down to the Lerry Market on Wednesday and Saturday mornings.

Father Joseph Matlenga, pastor of St. Albertus, recalled his father cutting limbs off trees and decorating the outside of their house on Pentecost.

And during the Corpus Christi celebration, three homes would be chosen for outside altars. "That was an honor," he said, "to be chosen for an altar."

All three parishes supported schools, and in 1921, according to Father Matlenga, 2,500 Polish-American children were enrolled at St. Albertus alone.

Without exception, observers attribute the viability of the churches and their schools to the Poles' intense loyalty to their parishes and to their national heritage.

The immediate needs of their church and the Polish community were of paramount importance to them, despite the penury wrought by two intense depressions during the life of the three churches, built late in the 19th Century.

Need itself forged a warm kinship among the people of Poletown.

"I remember when my father got a raise to $1 an hour," Father Poznanski reflected. "That was a great victory for our family. And we all shared in the joy of that victory."

Clara Swieczkowska, 80, the articulate former editor of the Polish Daily Record, recalled the "golden years" of Poletown from her home on E. Forest, where she has lived for the past 68 years.

Disabled by a broken hip that never healed after a fall almost a decade ago, she is now confined to her home.

Intensely proud of the Polish people, of their heritage and of her accomplishments as a lay worker for the church, Miss Clara—as friends call her—paints a portrait of their purposeful commitment to bettering the Polish community.

"My people never worked for themselves," she said of her parents. "They worked for the Polish cause. My father didn't have time for anything but Poland.

"People were all neighbors or all friends. Or if they had a fight, they wouldn't go to court; they would go to the rectory."

Father Matlenga explained that his father worked in the car shop at "Ford's" for meager wages. Nevertheless, the two things that were "of utmost importance" to his father, Matlenga said, were tuition for his children to attend Catholic school, and pew rent.

"As kids we didn't know the difference," he said. "We ate good because my mother would make bean soup with potatoes, or cherry soup.

"But I remember whenever that tuition was due, or that pew rent, my father would say: 'Make sure we pay it right away.'

"Some of these families originally mortgaged their homes to finance the building of this church (Sweetest Heart of Mary)," Father Poznanski said. "How many people would do that today? And if a man wanted to, would his wife allow him? Or vice versa? Today if it happened, it would make the news. Then, it was a common practice."

The Industrial Revolution transformed the face of Europe and America. Less workers were needed on farms as new machinery greatly multiplied production. Rural Europeans searched for jobs anywhere they could find them. Attracted by great economic opportunity in highly industrialized Chicago, Czech people left their native province of Bohemia (in 1918 to become Czechoslovakia).

The Czechs in Chicago

Half a century has passed since Bohemians first crossed the ocean, and after a long and dreaded journey and much uncertainty, settled down in Chicago, which was then scarcely more than a large village on the Lake shore in the endless prairie.

Today, Chicago is the third largest Bohemian city in the world, having about one hundred thousand Bohemians, grouped in several colonies of which "Pilsen" is the largest. Originally, the Bohemians lived on Van Buren and Canal streets where now rushing business life is focused. But these settlers were accustomed to villages and small rustic towns, where they cultivated their fields and lived by their handicraft. Therefore, they soon moved from their first seats near the lake and, when the influx of Jews and Italians

Excerpted from Alice G. Masaryk, "The Bohemians in Chicago," *Charities* (December 3, 1904), pp. 206–210.

If some older ethnic settlements are dissolving, others, such as this Cuban neighborhood in Miami, are forming. Courtesy Wide World Photos.

into their new quarters began to change the character of the settlement, they moved again. The growth of Pilsen thus began after 1870, and after thirty years shows a certain crystallization of what is typical and characteristic of Bohemian-American life. The other quarters are of more recent date and in many respects bear to Pilsen the relation of colonies to a motherland.

• • •

The Bohemians at home have a strong family life. A married son or daughter remains under the same roof with the aged parents, who retire into a quiet nook, where they enjoy their flaxen-haired, brown-eyed grandchildren. This trait, though modified, continues in Chicago. On a Sunday afternoon, the Eighteenth street car is filled with families, scrubbed, brushed and starched-up, bound for some festival hall to have a good time.

The Bohemian housekeepers know how to get great results from small means, which is most valuable for the poorer class and shows in the red and glossy cheeks of the children. On the other hand, the heavy food (pork with dumplings, for instance, is very common, and with it the usual glass of beer) produces those of full forms without corresponding strength, so general among the well-to-do citizens.

The Bohemians are capable of being amalgamated quickly. They learn the language easily; they give work for which even under competition, they can demand decent wages; they take an interest in politics.

• • •

Two pages, large sheets of the daily paper *Svornost* lie before me, covered with small print, giving the names of Bohemian clubs, societies, and lodges in Chicago. The Catholic press gives another long list of Catholic lodges, Catholic clubs. This fever for organization is typical of the Bohemians in Chicago. It was forty years ago that the few Bohemian settlers started their first club, the "Slavic Limetree." This beginning was simple, and almost idyllic. "We ought to have a little church for our grandmothers," one of the members suggested a little later. "A church where they could pray their *pater noster* in peace and then we'll be fixed. If we had a mill on the river I should think that we were in Bohemia."

The grandmothers received their church—no small gift in those times. It cost much enthusiasm and good will. Since that simple beginning, many activities have been at work which have resulted in the social organization—the work of individuals, of masses.

• • •

The emigration consists almost entirely of working people of whom it has been shown a large percentage is skilled handworkers. It must be borne in mind that while within the last fifty years, centralization of capital and subdivision of labor have reached an unparalleled height in America, in Bohemia, the old guild system which prevailed for centuries is slowly dying off through the same process. The old settlers, who came forty years ago and filled their stores with homemade goods (in those times one tailor flourished alongside of another on Nineteenth street) look amazed on the newcomers and shake their heads: "The idea of an eight-hour day." "The idea of strikes." The once independent handworkers become foremen in great establishments, cutters in tailor shops, butchers in stock yards, workers in the lumber yards, and a great many become shop-keepers. The middle class naturally dreads the great industrial revolution and hates with equal zest trusts and trade unions. But in the trade union movement the Bohemian workman, like all other intelligent working people, takes a part. And in Chicago, the unions with a Bohemian administration (over twenty in number) have a Bohemian central body.

A large factor in the industrial life is the fact that the Bohemians in Chicago practically have a third generation on this soil, though the first generation is still coming in. Therefore, it is natural that with the great thriftiness of the people and their desire to give their children a good education, Bohemians should be found in different branches of business as well as in all professions. In the home country brewing and the making of beet sugar are two of the oldest industries, and three breweries, founded by Bohemian capital, operate in Chicago, influencing the number of saloons not exactly to the benefit of the population.

The Bohemians have a tendency to own houses and so to have permanent homes. This tendency has been very much helped by the Subsidiary Loan Association. The first was started in 1870, and by 1902 there were over thirty Bohemian loan associations of this kind. Six percent is the highest rate of interest. Of the officers, only the secretary is paid and the books are revised once a year by a state officer. The system of mutual benefit societies has also taken on large dimensions. *Svornost* gives the name of sixteen orders, which in Chicago have 259 lodges. *Denni Hlasatal* gives about thirty Catholic associations and this is far from being a full list. These orders pay sick and death benefits, the business basis of the lodges being combined with a social element.

• • •

The social life among the Bohemians is very much alive. There are dances, concerts, theatrical performances. Since the Columbian Exposition a company of professional actors has resided in Pilsen, who on Sunday evenings play before a full house in the large hall, Thalia.

Besides the tendency to avail themselves of the unaccustomed freedom, other factors enter into the social life, such as the rivalry between the Catholics and Freethinkers, the rivalry of individuals, and the indirect economic interest. A new settler finds customers in the club or lodge he joins. This can be reduced *ad absurdum,* when, for instance, all the grocers from the district meet in the same club with the same intention. The educational element is of great importance. I was struck by the cleverness and efficiency with which the Bohemian women conduct their meetings. The men gain here a training for political life.

Other than these mutual benefit organizations, you will find all kinds of societies especially among the Freethinkers, such as turner (gymnastic) clubs (35), singing clubs (18), printing clubs (7), bicycle clubs (5), dramatic clubs (4) and many others.

The Bohemians are born musicians. "Where is the Bohemian who does not love music?" is a cadence in Smetana's music which says everything. You will find on the West Side many music schools, many violinists and pianists, amateurs, besides the professional musicians who have three unions.

A large park near Dunning, a beautiful garden, is the Bohemian cemetery. Its beginning belongs to the time of the separation of the Freethinkers from the Catholic Church. A Catholic priest refused to bury in the Catholic cemetery a woman who died without a confession, and the Freethinkers resolved to have a cemetery of their own. Like the Catechism of Freethinking, this cemetery proclaims how deeply the roots of Catholic logic and way of thinking penetrated the Bohemian soul. The great pomp with which the dead are buried by Freethinkers belongs to the middle ages, to the shadows of cathedrals. It is touching to watch the pride with which they love this piece of American soil. All the thoughts and memories of their old home, that are so dear to them, seem to be thought more easily and better in this garden of the dead, for something died within them when they left their homes. The pure memory lives as the memory of those who have left them forever and sleep under that velvety grass, under the brightest autumn leaves and the faithful asters.

What Are Working-Class Ethnic Neighborhoods Like?

Working-class ethnic neighborhoods are inhabited by immigrants or the descendants of immigrants who came to the cities of America during the great waves of migrations after 1890. In the eyes of city planners and developers they are sometimes considered unsightly gray areas that should be shoved aside by bulldozers so that "attractive" town houses and superhighways may brighten up the city.

Although doctors, lawyers, teachers, judges, and businessmen live in these sections, the majority of residents make their living by working with their hands. They are employed in transportation, manufacturing, and construction industries and range from being highly skilled craftsmen to unskilled laborers.

Many writers have ignored the ethnic diversity within cities. They assumed that the immigrants, after improving their lot, moved away from their "foreign colonies" and dispersed into "nicer" neighborhoods, to mix with the older "native" population. You will read about three ethnic neighborhoods which served as primary, or first, settlements for newcomers to the city. Italian-Americans sold their wares at the 9th Street Market in the 1880s mainly to fellow countrymen pouring into Philadelphia. St. Patrick's parish in Schuylkill sent young Irish off to the Union Army, and South Street came under scrutiny by the famous black social scientist W.E.B. DuBois in his first book, *Philadelphia Negro,* in 1899.

While the three readings describe neighborhoods in one city, these areas have their counterparts in New York, Detroit, Cleveland, Chicago, and other urban centers.

For each of the descriptions that follow (1) List the factors that pull or keep residents in an area; (2) Identify the characteristics of lifestyle—holidays, customs, and such—of each.

Little Italy in Philadelphia

Part One: Many Still Swear by 9th St. Market

The 9th st. Market in South Philadelphia wakes up soon after dawn every day.

As the first faint streaks of sunlight paint the dull dirty sky, old trucks—beat-up trucks—rumble up narrow 9th st. to deliver produce fresh from the farms of New Jersey.

By mid-morning, the teeming streets are alive with color and litter and with people. Freshly slaughtered suckling pigs hang, stark and white, from hooks outside one shop. Down the street, under awnings faded by a generation of hot sun, live Maryland crabs are for sale. They grope and snap in their baskets.

The market is one of those Philadelphia phenomena, a neighborhood center that grew from the old-country ways of the Italians and the Jews and was handed down to their children. Today, despite the antiseptic chains of standardized supermarkets, many Philadelphians still swear by this ramshackle old market. Many still like the feel, the excitement and the reality of it.

In a sawdust-floored meat shop on 9th st., a butcher named Tony put it this way: "A lot of these people never go near a supermarket. They like to see and feel what they buy. You don't know you're getting good meat every time in some store where they cut it and wrap it in the cellar.

You could tell by the way Tony the Butcher displayed a nice roast and cut it that he was proud of his profession, a butcher among butchers.

People like that make the 9th st. Market what it is.

Part One, "Many Still Swear by 9th St. Market," is by Joe Sharkey, reprinted by permission of the *Philadelphia Inquirer,* September 25, 1970.

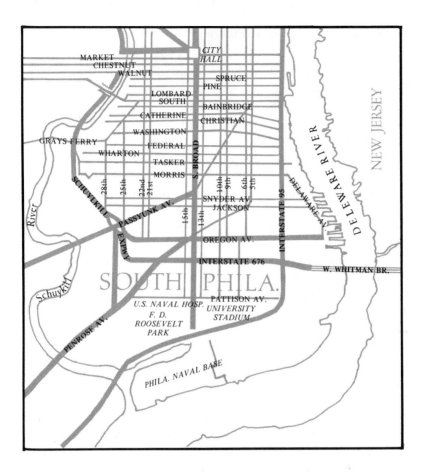

Part Two: Love in a Small Town Called South Philadelphia

Garry Iaconelli, twenty-one, a South Philadelphia soldier, returned from war last week. He got the kind of greeting his neighborhood is noted for. Strung across the block were red, white, and blue
pennants. Outside his family's house at 740 South 8th street was an
18-by-25-foot banner: "Welcome Home My Son from Vietnam."

Adapted from Walter Naedele, "Step Sitting Takes You into the
Past," *Philadelphia Bulletin,* July 23, 1971; also Peter Binzen, "There's
Plenty of Love in That Small Town Called South Philadelphia,"
Neighborhoods of Philadelphia (pamphlet), (Philadelphia: Philadelphia
Bulletin Company, 1969).

Inside, Garry's father, Joseph, a longshoreman, his mother Lena, who hadn't read the papers or watched television for a month because she feared the worst, his married older brother and married sister, his five aunts and two uncles and thirty-one cousins threw their arms around him and told him how wonderful it was to have him back. The relatives were sure to be there, for Italian families are very close.

The remarkable thing about this outpouring of warmth and affection for a returned loved one was that in South Philadelphia it goes on all the time. To many people South Philly still seems like a small town. That explains why they love it. Garry's father walks to work on the waterfront and his mother walks to 7 A.M. Mass at St. Mary Magdalen Depazzi Church, the oldest Italian church in North America. She walks also to nearby grocery and cheese stores.

Italian women attend church much more than the men. Most Italian males receive baptism, confirmation, and First Holy Communion, but after that many rarely appear in church until their death. The women attend mass often, regularly on Sunday morning, and admit their sins to a priest in a confessional booth on Saturday afternoon.

Italian people believe it is very important to honor a person properly upon death. Italian families in South Philadelphia will, if necessary, mortgage their homes and pawn the silverware to give their dead a funeral that is at least as grand or more so than the one down the block a week before. At the services mourners cry out in anguish, shed many tears in front of the casket, and leave many Mass cards [notice that Mass is to be offered for the deceased] at the altar.

Another characteristic of the residents of this "town within a city" is the great pride Italo-Americans put in their homes. Neat, modest row houses give little external evidence of sumptuous renaissance interiors. The insides appear rather feminine with lace and bric-a-brac all around. Most rooms seem dressed for guests, to show off how tasteful a housewife the lady of the house is. The decor of the furniture, railings, and wallpaper is Mediterranean. Many homes boast over 140 years of use, yet contain the most up-to-date modern appliances and conveniences. Practically all of the labor for the modernization came from the hands of the owner and his rela-

Shopping in specialty stores is a part of life in ethnic neighborhoods.

tives. Italians have skilled hands; they are well represented in the building trades. Three generations of men and women have pampered the house.

Recreation has an ethnic side. Italian-American men meet in their mummers' clubs for all sorts of activities. All year long they drill, gather funds, prepare costumes, march, and practice musical numbers for the big day—the annual New Year's Mummers' Parade. The competition consists mainly of the Irish-Americans of Kensington and the Polish-American Club of Richmond.

Young and old mix at the playgrounds, small squares that lightly pepper South Philadelphia. At the Guerin Playground, located where 16th meets Jackson, the oldsters play on what appears to be the only indoor bocci court in the country. Bocci is the Italian version of bowling, only with lighter and smaller balls. On the benches some grandfathers can be seen playing checkers with their grandchildren, while others watch a softball game. The bocci court at Broad and Federal sits beside a basketball hoop, and the older men playing outdoors have some trouble quieting down the black and white young basketball players yelling near them.

Indoor fun can be found at the Victor Cafe, 1303 Dickinson Street, where the patrons can down spaghetti while listening to arias from one of the finest recorded musical collections in the city. Whatever the customer requests in the way of classical music, the host at Victor's plays. Often a patron will break out with a song; hearing a pleasant tenor voice comes as no surprise in this neighborhood.

This neighborhood has had amazing staying power. Despite some leakage—that is, the moving away of residents to the suburbs—many young Italian-Americans remain in the district. Some make their homes as far south as Oregon Avenue. They don't want to leave this "urban village," this community of close friends and neighbors, this colorful area of active street life and home life.

A Little Irish Village in Center City

It sits at the foot of the South Street bridge, a small neighborhood, only a few square blocks. It looks like a lot of other places in Philadelphia with long, solid rows of two- or three-story weathered brick houses, none very wide, on narrow streets made even narrower by parked cars.

The Delaware Valley is filled with people who don't even know it exists. From a casual glance on the way to the expressway, it doesn't look like a place you'd be dying to move into. But if you ask somebody from 26th and South or Bambry and Bainbridge where they live, they don't say Center City or South Philadelphia. The answer comes promptly and proudly, "Schuylkill," always pronounced "Skookil."

Surrounded by affluent Center City, decaying South Street, the Naval Home, and the Schuylkill River, Schuylkill is an almost all-Irish working class enclave. Most residents own their own homes. These neat, modest houses, assessed at $19,000 to $23,000, stand amidst garages, small factories, warehouses, and oil-storage tanks. The residents don't mind it. Inside the occupants live surrounded by a decor that is like a page out of the 1930s. Dark wooden furniture and bric-a-brac dominate the ground floor of a well-used

Adapted from Rem Rieder, "Schuylkill: A Little Irish Village Tucked into Center City," *Neighborhoods of Philadelphia* (pamphlet), Philadelphia: Philadelphia Bulletin Company, 1969), pp. 27–28.

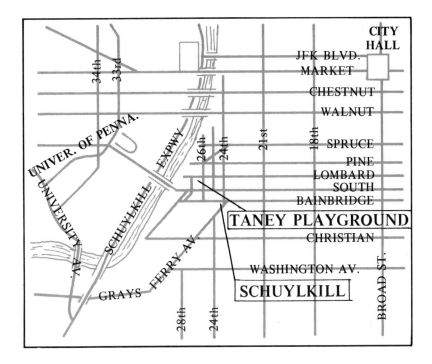

kitchen and rarely used dining room and living room. In the living room opposite the door a statue of Jesus looks over the scene from His fixed position on the wall. On the kitchen wall a religious calendar noted with all the Catholic holy days and saints' days under the Savior's bearded face peers into the room.

Most families in Schuylkill seem to be related to the other families in Schuylkill. In the midst of a fragmented, uptight, lonely city, its 150 families have established among themselves a feeling of community. As young Eddie McBride points out, "In Schuylkill everybody knows everybody else. Families live here for generations. My grandparents lived here and so do my parents. Families just don't move out."

"It's the kind of neighborhood where if you get sick, you know your neighbor will take care of you," says Tessie Callahan, the wife of the owner of Callahan's Tavern, 2615 South Street. "It's like little Ireland, a little village."

It is becoming increasingly difficult for many of these working class families to move away, for the income of $11,000 to $14,000 that most breadwinners make could not take them into the suburbs, where the going rate on carefully zoned houses starts near $40,000 to $55,000.

Schuylkill's residents are not joiners. While some belong to the American Legion Post 803, McCooley, Hannon, and Lavin, most use the neighborhood taverns as community meeting places. Callahan's Tavern is located at Taney and South streets, Gavin's at 24th and Lombard, Mileen's at 26th and Pine.

On a windy fall afternoon a visitor stops into Callahan's, which has been owned by the Callahan family for thirty-three years. It is a big, comfortable place with a homelike atmosphere. The bar is packed, and at one table a beefy guy is eating lunch. At another Tom Callahan Senior is playing cards with his cronies. Callahan gets a friend to play out his hand and starts to talk to a visitor. While some talk is about sports and current affairs, a great deal of the conversation is about work. Schuylkill's men work at blue-collar jobs and are well represented in the building trades. Following an old Irish tradition, police officers and firemen make their homes here too. Over at Gavin's Bar the emphasis is often on the shuffleboard machine; stop in on a weekday night and you're apt to see intense competition among the young men of the neighborhood. Another attraction is an outstanding rock jukebox.

For those too young to congregate in taverns the central meeting place is Cass Morgan's candy store at 26th and South. (Schuylkill does not have a full-fledged hoagie shop.) It is an old-fashioned candy store, the kind where kids come in and buy a nickel or dime's worth of gumdrops. On the wall are pictures of neighborhood kids and a map of Ireland.

Sports are very important in the Schuylkill scene. Neighborhood institutions like Gavin's sponsor football and softball teams in leagues at Taney Playground, Taney and Pine streets. A lot of basketball is played at the University House at 26th and Lombard. Many Schuylkill hoop hotshots have been tutored by Jim O'Connor, a neighborhood legend known to many as "Mr. Schuylkill."

Schuylkill is almost 100 percent Irish—some families are only half Irish—and is staunchly Roman Catholic. Residents living on the north side of South Street go to St. Patrick's Church at 20th and Locust streets. Those to the south go to St. Anthony's, 24th Street and Grays Ferry Avenue. Almost all the kids attend parochial

Neighborhood taverns and local parks are community meeting places and sources of recreation for residents.

schools. Parents send them despite high tuition costs because they want their children to have religious training and because they feel that the parochial school will provide more discipline.

The church is important to this tightly knit community. Both men and women regularly attend services as well as the charitable and social affairs that revolve about the church. The older generation tends to be quite conservative and looks unfavorably at recent changes occurring in this 2000-year-old institution.

Patriotism is not out-of-date with the residents. Many houses have flags and flag decals in the windows. Parents of draft-age sons, while not happy with the Vietnam war, nevertheless are proud of their son's military service, and draft dodging is not a popular subject.

Schuylkill remains a dwindling enclave of traditional home life as a wave of center-city young, rather well-off white people, move in from the north, while poor blacks move in from the east. Its sandwiched-in location between the river and the large naval home accounts for its relatively unchanged way of life, but it is anybody's guess how long this "village" can hold out.

Take Your Bulldozer Somewhere Else Whitey!

I used to live in another world only four blocks away from South Street, the world of white center city. And my landlady, who had an apartment with white walls, white linoleum, white furniture, a white piano, and even a white dog, was distressed when she discovered that she had one nonwhite item in the building. Me.

But that wasn't the main reason why I moved from Pine Street. I was lonely and frightened there—I think all single people in center city are lonely and frightened—and down here near South Street I'm not.

The guys on South Street are friendly; they really don't want a date with you. They already have a wife at home, plus an extra woman on the side who's making life sufficiently complicated for them. What they *do* want is a chance to express themselves and to have their self-expression acknowledged by a *response,* if it's only a smile. After all, on Chestnut Street nobody even notices them. Down here, in their home territory, they demand to be recognized.

If you don't smile when spoken to or say, "How do you do" or "Good Evening" (there's a curious formality of speech down here), the immediate verdict, announced for all to hear, is that you think you are cute. To think you're cute is the kiss of death on South Street. But nobody's going to kill you for it. There are too many distractions, including a hundred other women coming along behind you.

A stroll on South Street is a series of friendly, homey exchanges, not all with flirtatious men. An elderly codger declares as I pass him, "Yep, you're out walking today, Missy. You're really out walking." No reply can possibly be framed, or is, for that matter, expected: just smile and move on.

Adapted from Kristin Hunter, "Report from South Street," *Philadelphia Magazine* (August, 1967), pp. 92–94, 96–97.

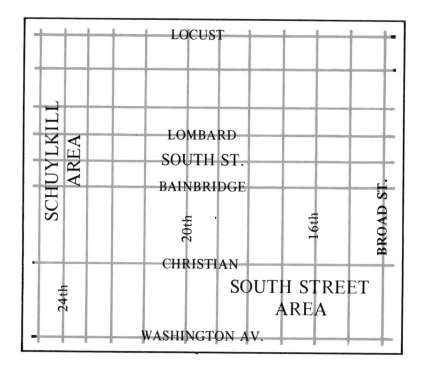

The style of life is leisurely and warm because South Street people are essentially *Southern*—country folks who retain their rural ways—gentle good humor, good manners, a slow pace, and a forthright manner with strangers that is not so much freshness as a hometown *friendliness* that makes them want to know everybody in the neighborhood and be known in return.

There's also a wide streak of courtliness, a positive aristocratic gentility, that crops up at the oddest times. There are ten "Good evening, madams" for every "Hey, baby." The housewife with a dozen kids to watch who also keeps a vigilant eye on my (white and colored) friends' cars when they are parked on her block. The absolutely frightening-looking character, razor-scarred, wild-haired, and toothless, who springs to pick up my change if I drop it on the sidewalk—and refuses to accept any of it in thanks. The forty guys who work for my landlords, the garage downstairs. One and all, they tip their hats when they see me or any other woman known to them. They are happy to unstop drains or lug parcels upstairs or provide any other assistance needed by a helpless female. And just let an unwanted caller try to gain entrance. There's more muscle down there, and more willing gallantry, than you'd find in a brigade of fancy doormen.

Yes, I'll miss South Street. I have just gotten married and my husband has some plans to live near his work. I'll miss:

Secondhand shoes, not only a boon to the poor, but a blessing to victims of fashion whose bunions and corns make it agony to break in a new pair. And if your secondhand shoes are a bit too beat-up, nearby is a shoemaker who charges only $1.25 for heels and $3.00 for half soles. I'll miss:

The upholsterer who's redoing three chairs for me, capably and lovingly, for a grand total of $150 plus fabric. Wanamakers, Gimbel's, I defy you to compete!

The old lady with an outdoor stand near 15th Street displaying huge horehound and peppermint sticks and all sorts of fresh and dried herbs.

The enterprising young man on another corner who sells freshly opened clams in season.

A 24-hour grocery store for emergencies. Fresh fish, fruit, and vegetable stores in every block.

Tasty Southern specialties like sage sausage, ham hocks, pigs' feet, and whole grains, also in every block.

Hot-roasted peanuts, a big bag for 85 cents.

The barbeque shops and the fried-shrimp and chicken stores open 24 hours a day—a handy compromise for days when you don't feel like cooking or like getting dressed up to face a center-city restaurant.

The definitely casual-dress restaurant near 18th, with trays of homemade rolls in the window that only hint at the other delights inside.

I'll miss South Street for these conveniences.

I'll also miss the sidewalk performances of street blues and gospel singers, and the store-front churches with their astonishing musicians.

I'll miss the garden of the Church of God and the Saints of Christ (definitely not a store-front) on Broad just below South, lovingly tended by lady volunteers. Right now it is garlanded with roses, hydrangeas, zinias and four-o'clocks which provide decor for the church's annual outdoor barbeque.

I'll miss the COGASOC choir, too—at least a hundred superb voices exquisitely blended by a skilled director blown to my ears free each week.

I'll miss the constant background of miscellaneous music, all good, authentic rhythm-and-blues and gospel, from radios and record shops and impromptu performers.

I'll miss the guys in red and purple sport shirts, the gals in orange and green raincoats, the kids in pink and yellow dresses, vivid colors that go well with their vivid skins.

I'll miss the Black Muslims politely peddling propaganda and calling me "Sister," and the churchgoers who call me the same thing (I was an only child).

I won't miss the fumes and soot of South Philadelphia, but I will miss, when the wind blows the other way, the scent of my own petunias growing on what may be South Philadelphia's largest roof garden. And I'll miss the guys who gather nightly in the alley below my roof to croon ballads. (They can't see me, but I can hear them. And they're *good.*)

Along with the other things I have mentioned, I'll miss the constant background hum of voices never heard in silent white neighborhoods.

I'll miss the permanent forum of old men on the corner of Broad and South, intensely arguing the world's problems as if it were up to them, and only them, to solve them.

What I'll miss most of all about South Street is the human qualities, its warmth, its friendliness, its interest and concern for others, qualities increasingly rare in detached urban America.

Important Public Issues Grow Out of Ethnic Group Togetherness

Shall Ethnic Neighborhoods Be Destroyed in the Name of Progress?

You have read of ethnic neighborhoods and the satisfactions residents receive by living in them. Too often in the eyes of city planners and redevelopers they are viewed in terms of aged housing, high-population density, and mixed land uses, meaning the presence of small factories, warehouses, garages, and stores peppered among residential houses. In the name of progress—new superhighways, more fashionable housing, expansion of commercial and industrial facilities—ethnic neighborhoods may be wiped out. The author of the reading to follow calls this process "ethnocide."

"The New Ethnocide" brings out a conflict over two values: the social goals of planners who offer as their motives the broader needs of the city as opposed to the needs of one social group and its desire to survive and preserve its way of life. Is there a solution? *When you complete the reading, think of a solution and how you would justify it.*

The New Ethnocide

by Nancy Seifer*

In the case of the Northside of Williamsburg vs. the City of New York, the people have charged the Mayor with ethnocide—the

*Reprinted with permission from *The Village Voice* (February 15, 1973). Copyrighted © by The Village Voice, Inc., 1973.

systematic destruction of an ethnic community and its culture. The nomenclature may be new, but the phenomenon is not. The Northside has, in fact, been dubbed another Corona. It is another example of ruinous city "planning" which eradicates viable communities.

Last November, 40 families and two small businesses on the Northside, a predominantly Polish-American community, received eviction notices from the City of New York. Those on North 4th Street had until April 30 and those on North 3rd until June 30 to get out—to leave the homes in which many had spent their whole lives, in favor of the expansion of S&S Corrugated Paper Machinery Company. "It's an unbelievable case of cardboard taking precedence over flesh and blood," said Lilly Manisseri, who helped save Corona's 69 homes from the jaws of the bulldozer three years ago.

Since November, the Northside has been geared up to "battle to the death." Working-class people who never dreamed of "sitting in" found themselves linking arms to block rush-hour traffic on the Brooklyn-Queens Expressway, armed with picket signs that read: "Mayor Lindsay has a home, what about us?" and "If you want industrial expansion, take Gracie Mansion."

"I was petrified," said 52-year-old Mrs. Anastasi Zawadzki McGuinness, a leader of the fight to save the homes, who has lived in the community all her life, along with two brothers, their families, and her mother, who died two weeks ago. "That was the first time we ever did anything like that in our lives. But it's amazing what you can get yourself to do if it means survival."

To many people, the entire saga of the Northside is symbolic of a dehumanized city government, which views people as rootless atoms to be juggled around at will. It is symptomatic of a bureaucracy which seems to have gone berserk—which demolishes sound housing with none to replace it, and annihilates crime-free communities while pouring more millions into new crime-prevention programs.

The fate of 85 families on the Northside (half have already moved) was sealed behind closed doors sometime before 1969, when S&S Corrugated threatened to desert New York City with 400 or so jobs to expand in the greener industrial pastures of New Jersey. The Economic Development Administration rushed to the rescue, so the story goes, and made the company an offer it couldn't refuse—help in getting any land it needed for its expansion. In return, S&S would remain and eventually add a few hundred more employes to its payroll, for an eventual total of about 700—nothing to sneeze at.

On the face of it, EDA performed admirably. The only problem was, on the two blocks which were generously offered to S&S lived 85 families whose lifestyle and cultural traditions date back to the arrival of their parents, many of whom came to the U.S. from countries like Poland, the Ukraine, Lithuania, Italy, and Germany to escape the tyranny of Stalin, Hitler, or Mussolini.

"What about democracy?" asked Mrs. Anna Zawadzki. "Our parents came here to be free and make a decent living for their children. They built the country. Now we can't even live where we want."

"Our kids have gone to Vietnam to fight," said Mrs. McGuinness, her sister-in-law. "My husband fought in World War II, in Korea, and now he's a disabled veteran with no job. Now look what they're doing to us. The city expects people to completely change their way of life after 50 years in one place. No one has the right to do that."

Whether or not the city has the right to do that will be tested in the courts by a team of volunteer lawyers for the community, including newly appointed Councilman Fred Richmond. Nowhere in the City Charter is it written that the city has the right to condemn property for the sake of a profit-making corporation. It does have the right to condemn property for the "public good," and no one would dispute that 500 jobs are good for the city. The problem resulted from our city fathers' callous disregard for human lives, and the lack of any rational planning. Also, as a number of officials have said off the record, the pressure from the community came too late. "They should have begun screaming three years ago," said one.

The people of North 3rd and 4th Streets first learned of the plan to raze their homes when Rudy Stobierski, community leader, member of the local planning board, and owner of a neighborhood funeral parlor, rang their doorbells one evening in May 1969, with the latest edition of the Daily News in hand.

What followed was a series of City Planning Commission and

Older row houses such as these in an ethnic neighborhood are often the victims of urban redevelopment.

Board of Estimate hearings. The first, attended by well over 400 people, was held at Our Lady of Consolation Church, where it became clear that the die was already cast. The re-zoned map of the area presented to the people showed their homes blackened out, with the extension of S&S in their place.

The people were powerless. They had never been organized, but had traditionally turned to the local priest or politicians for help. "Maybe if we had organized we might have saved the area," Reverend Bundy of Our Lady of Consolation Church said recently, "but a lot of this was done behind the scenes and we weren't even conscious of it."

In a crunch with government, the people asked their elected officials for help. "They put on a good act," one resident said. "They all got up and made flowery speeches. They offered their condolences, and kept saying 'we'll try' as we were being buried alive."

"The best thing to come out of all this is that we got wise," said another. "We've learned you can't trust most of them. It'll be murder for the next one of that bunch who tries to get elected. They never had to do anything and they kept getting re-elected. They had it too good."

The hearings were held, the people protested in whatever way they knew how, but they were not organized and they lost. On December 4, 1969, the Board of Estimate passed a resolution permitting S&S Corrugated to proceed with its plans for expansion, and the gears of city machinery were set into motion to condemn the property and prepare for relocation, eviction, and demolition. "It's a crime to demolish these homes," said a Department of Relocation official who wished to remain anonymous. "Usually, the ones we get rid of are loaded with violations and the people are happy to get out."

An obvious next question might be, what has the City of New York done to reward the Northside families for the sacrifice of their homes and their way of life?

First, the residents were awarded between $9000 and $14,000 for their homes—far less than they would have gotten on the open market (according to relocation officials) and far less than they would have gotten if the area had not been zoned manufacturing (according to City Planning officials). Obviously, no equivalent housing exists in this city at that price.

Second, the city never bothered to comply with its own relocation statutes. Plans for providing comparable housing in the area which are supposed to be submitted before condemnation proceedings begin, somehow never materialized. At the 1969 hearings, there was talk of new vest-pocket and renovated housing in the neighborhood. Ken Patton and his assistants recently began to talk of plans for local relocation, to everyone except the residents themselves. The Housing and Development Administration, however, claims no such plans exist. "There's no actual plan," said one official. "We have our regular finder's fee program and we try to give them priority in public housing projects, in Queens or somewhere, but they don't seem to want to go." Even S&S could not defend EDA on this issue.

Of the 45 families who have already relocated, six were assisted by the Department of Relocation. One was an elderly woman, moved to a housing project, where she was mugged and robbed twice in three weeks. Said Mrs. McGuinness, "They're going to kill me first before they put me in public housing. That's not our way of life."

Thirty of the families found housing in the Northside. There is virtually none left, especially at $50 or $60 a month, which some of the families now pay and which is all they can afford.

Lastly, the residents may have lost out on the only hope for a proper financial reward for their sacrifice. If the homeowners had lived in a federal instead of a city urban renewal area, they would have received a subsidy of up to $15,000, in addition to the condemnation price, to find equivalent housing. HDA is currently writing the rules and regulations for a similar city plan, and has requested an increase in relocation funds in the current budget for that purpose. But again, so they say, it's too late for the Northsiders who are no longer homeowners. They were forced to sell their homes to the city, to whom they now pay rent. (The city, it appears, would rather keep the new plan secret, for fear of a Pandora's box.)

"The city is showing us and our kids that it doesn't pay to obey the law," said one woman. "What do you get for it? My mother always said if you don't make no trouble, you get no trouble. But it's not true. You get it even when you don't make it."

The people on the Northside, with the help of Jan Peterson, an extraordinary community organizer who came out of the civil rights movement and Mobilization for Youth (without whom, they all say, they don't know where they'd be today), have gotten politically wise and organized. The kind of wisdom they've gained is power. They are prepared for a long fight, with the help of a crew of volunteer lawyers, who have already made several state court appearances and will go to federal court if need be; and planners from Pratt Institute's Center for Community and Environmental Development, who are working on feasible alternative housing plans for the residents to remain in the existing "social neighborhood," on possible alternatives for S&S, and on plans to re-zone the area for mixed residential and manufacturing use, to assure its future viability.

Northsiders are also aware that S&S is pulling everyone's leg, that it had bought some land in New Jersey in the 1960s, tried unsuccessfully to lure its workers out there (to the point of busing them out for tours and Saturday night parties), that the land they bought turned out to be swamp, and that the city, in fact, rescued it from a huge economic loss.

They also understand that their own tax dollars are paying for the $4.2 million low-interest loan which S&S received (with the help of Congressman John Rooney) on the grounds that it was "keeping employment in a distressed area"; and for the destruction of their own homes.

At City Hall there is mostly dead silence, broken occasionally with murmurings of "looking into it." At the Housing and Development Administration, where the Northsiders went to see Andrew Kerr about what the City had done over the three years between condemnation and eviction to provide comparable housing in the neighborhood, they were told by Kerr to see Ken Patton, who Kerr said had helped S&S get the loan. Last week, John Scanlon, Patton's spokesman at EDA, muttered sanctimoniously about what a difficult decision it was, how they had to weigh the needs of 500 families (probably a high estimate of the current number of S&S employes) against the needs of 40 families, quoted statistics which even S&S denied were true, admitted to having no knowledge about the city's responsibility for relocating the families, and suggested (to complete the vicious cycle) that this writer find out from HDA.

And so, one wonders, what about the people: What about the 82-year-old woman with arthritis who cries herself to sleep every night because she has no place to go? What about the known fact that uprooting elderly people can take at least five years off their lives? What about the woman who has had special facilities built into her home for her daughter who has polio? Where could the family with six kids afford to move? One wonders if anyone with the power to help really gives a damn.

Why Is Busing for Integration
a Thorny Issue?

No other issue has evoked such controversy as the school busing plan to integrate education. In 1954 the Supreme Court ruled in its famous *Brown* versus *Board of Education of Topeka* case that legal separation of blacks from whites in segregated schools violated the United States Constitution. Blacks were not receiving "equal protection of the law," a phrase from the Fourteenth Amendment. The Court reasoned that all-black schools were inherently (by their nature) unequal. Since then the South has made great strides in desegregating its schools. However, because of housing patterns the North has many *de facto* (by fact, but not by law) segregated schools. Resistence to plans to integrate Northern schools has been great, particularly to any project to take children out of their neighborhood schools.

As summer 1971 approached in San Francisco, the U.S. District Court serving that region agreed with a suit filed in behalf of black children attending school. The court ordered a busing plan for integration that would take San Francisco away from the tradition of having neighborhood schools. The strongly ethnic community of Chinatown reacted against this ruling by appealing to the U.S. Supreme Court. What follows are two accounts in newspaper form, prepared by the author and based on news stories of the time, that summarize two positions on this matter—integrationist and separatist (allowing an ethnic group to remain apart). *Note the arguments presented by both sides. What inferences can you make from the accounts? Do you agree with Justice Douglas's decision in this case? Explain.*

Three generations of Chinese Americans are represented at a busy street crossing in San Francisco's Chinatown. Preserving its ethnic identity is one of the prime concerns of the Chinese-American community. Courtesy Wide World Photos.

Chinese in San Francisco Protest School Busing Ruling

Chinese parents, represented by their lawyer Quentin Kopp, appealed to the U.S. Supreme Court to block massive busing of Chinese-American children from their neighborhood schools. They claimed that reassignment scheduled for the new school term in September was unconstitutional because the U.S. District Court order requiring transfer was based solely on race. Kopp claims "the law must be color blind."

The court-ordered plan would affect thousands of the 47,000 elementary children in San Francisco's 102 schools, 6,500 of them Chinese-American. White groups have also been threatening boycott of the city's public school system. However, the Chinese have been pleading a special need.

The Chinese Parents' Committee said they were determined to preserve their heritage, and they maintained that busing will destroy their community's pattern of life and culture. Members claimed that the neighborhood school system gave their children the opportunity to obtain an education in the Chinese language, art, and culture through additional facilities, centers maintained by the Chinese community. This enriched program begins at the end of the school day.

"If Chinese children are forced to travel long distances," they complain, "our community cultural centers will have to shut down because pupils will not be able to get to them on time."

About 50,000 of the city's 75,000 Chinese population live within the borders of Chinatown. Since the easing of immigration restrictions against Orientals with the passage of the Immigration Act of 1965, the population of the seventeen block area of Chinatown has grown by leaps and bounds. One member of the Parents' Committee expressed concern over the language barrier for young immigrants.

"What happens to a child five or eight years old who can't speak English well enough to talk? What happens if he is lost? He can't speak English well enough to say he is lost. We're worried about these kids who come over here and whom they want to ship out there."

One concerned parent, a pharmacist, observed that a major reason the Chinese are caught in the integration fight is that many Chinese have remained in the city while middle-class whites have fled to the suburbs. "It is no good to run," he stated determinedly. "Here we will make our stand."

Supreme Court Justice Rejects San Francisco Chinese Parents' Appeal

Justice William O. Douglas has rejected an appeal by Chinese parents fighting a Federal District Court plan for integration that would require children in Chinatown to be bused to schools outside their neighborhood.

The court order was in response to a suit brought by the National Association for the Advancement of Colored People (NAACP) which claimed that San Francisco's schools were racially unbalanced. The association contended that blacks were segregated in this bay city.   .

Proponents of integration argue that such segregation has a detrimental effect on the learning of black children by providing an unequal and inferior education for them. To prepare for life in a democratic society both blacks and whites must be exposed to a variety of cultures. Furthermore, integrationists contend that white society provides better schools for whites, so blacks mixed with whites receive this concern in the form of better teachers and facilities. They believe that black children learn better integrated and that this happens at no expense to the achievement of white children.

Supreme Court Justice Douglas based his rejection of the appeal by Chinese parents on an 1875 Supreme Court decision. The case involved the rights of laundryman Yick Wu. The ruling stated that neither the State of California nor San Francisco could deny Yick Wu a license to operate a hand laundry because he was Chinese. The case established a precedent for color-blind justice. According to Justice Douglas's view the principle growing out of this decision is that rights, laws, rulings, and court orders apply equally to all races. Douglas stated the U.S. District Court integration order applied equally to all San Francisco children regardless of racial or ethnic background. The Chinese were not being singled out.

TOPIC 16

Where Can Low-Cost Housing Be Built?

In the previous learning experience you learned of the resistence of Chinese-American residents to having their youngsters bused out. They considered this a threat to their pattern of life and culture. In Topic 14 residents of a working-class ethnic neighborhood saw a threat to their living patterns by erasing their buildings in favor of industrial expansion. The public issue of the location of public housing is another controversial one having ethnic and social-class overtones.

Under the regulations of the U.S. Department of Housing and Urban Development based on the 1968 Civil Rights Law, for every public-housing unit built in a predominately black neighborhood another must be built in a white one. Although this case study is fictional, the problems, circumstances, and comments are very real. The Bellevue Park Public Housing Project described is typical of the attempts to introduce low-cost housing for the poor (two-thirds white) into working-class neighborhoods in the city. This learning experience is in dialog form. *As you read the comments and examine the situation, what interests and values are coming into conflict? You should be able to recognize some of them from previous topics.*

The Situation

Bellevue Park was designed as a 300-unit, low-rise, two-story-homes, public-housing project. The units would be sold to occupants under a percent-of-income plan. It required that occupants maintain the properties. After twenty-one years residents would become owners. Residents close to the poverty level would receive

102

preference for occupancy. Welfare recipients could apply, and the utility cost would be waived when necessary. All taxes would be waived for ten years. The decision to build units in a condemned area in the middle of a working-class ethnic neighborhood was made by the City Housing Authority with moneys provided by the federal Housing and Urban Development agency (HUD). No consultation was sought with community organizations and leaders. When construction started on the project, neighborhood people calling themselves the Community Residents' Association effectively blocked the site and halted work.

Middle-Aged Neighborhood Resident:

People on welfare should not live in better houses than those who pay taxes. If people want a decent home, they should go out and work for it. This is a democracy, not a utopia. I break my back for a living. My house is the only real investment I have. Now, with this public housing the value of my house will go down, and my lifetime savings will disappear. I cannot afford to move. I've put plenty of sweat and money into making this house comfortable; a comparable home in the suburbs would cost too much. I like the neighbors here. We've known each other for years, belonged to the same church, helped each other out when in trouble. I am not against minorities coming; we've had colored people here in this neighborhood for years. They took care of their property and looked out after their kids, beat hell out of them like we do when they get out of line. We don't want people in here that will ruin the neighborhood. Let those professionals who planned this development put it in their own neighborhood!

Officer of City Housing Authority:

Opposition to the Bellevue Park Project is based on pure prejudice and racism. The outspoken members of the Community Residents' Association are taking council from their fears. They are convinced that occupants of these project homes will ruin their neighborhood and drag down their property values. They really fear desegregation. The government has a moral responsibility to rip down the wall of bigotry that has consigned minorities and the poor to second-class status in their own country. People don't want to live in public housing, but it is the only housing for the amount of money they have to pay. The poor must get out of ghettos created for them by the more affluent, for these ghettos mean inferior schooling, fewer jobs, rackets, dope pushing, and three times a greater chance to be robbed or burglarized. What does "community" or "neighborhood" mean? Is it the small area around the Bellevue site or this large metropolitan area? For the greater good we must break urban ghettos, both black and white. We deplore the open defiance of the law by the Community Residents' Association, which is rejecting the city's legal right to provide public housing.

Lawyer for Community Residents' Association:

These hard-working people have no restrictive zoning to protect their community. Nor does this state have a referendum law permitting communities to vote on the placement of public housing. What this association is fighting is the influx not of blacks, but of crime which is bred in poverty. The arrival of 1,000 or more low-income residents would overburden already overcrowded schools. Academic standards would drop; violence would rise. Purse snatching, mugging, and robberies would increase greatly, while women would fear going out at night. These new neighbors would not be committed to neighborhood stability. Oh, yes, the project will look beautiful the day before the first tenant moves in. But once these improvident enter, the ways of this community will change. The present residents keep up their little homes both inside and outside, share their joys and sorrows with friends on the street, share similar backgrounds—why, many have cultural traditions which date back to the arrival of their parents thirty to fifty years ago. These good people would be confronted with strangers who act differently. Our citizens know what happened to other neighborhoods in this city once public housing invaded, how invalid assurances of public officials were. This community has the right to preserve its identity.

Officer of the Agency of Housing and Urban Development:

Poor people are removed from areas near here. Where are they to live? Too often housing programs serving low-income groups have concentrated in ghettos. Federally aided low-income housing must be reoriented, so that the major thrust is in nonghetto areas. If this is not done, housing programs will continue to herd the most impoverished and dependent parts of the population into inner-city ghettos. As it is now, these sections suffer from the gap between the needs of the population—schools, playgrounds, health care, employment—and resources, both private and public, to deal with them. Low-cost housing in ghettos or inner-city locations can only compound the conditions of failure and hopelessness which lead to crime and social disorganization. Efforts have been made in Bellevue Park's plan to promote home ownership in the belief that with equity in their homes the new neighbors, although of low income, will take pride in them and be more stable residents.

Young Adult Neighborhood Resident:

All of us here do not think alike. I believe that poor people need a chance to better themselves. If the government can subsidize the rich, it can also help the poor. We cannot isolate ourselves from poverty and its problems. If something is not done, the problems of poverty will spread like a cancer all over the land; there is no escape. This community can absorb 1,000 low-income residents. It is good to learn how to get along with all kinds of people, not to stay always with your own kind. We should not prejudge anyone because of their income or skin color. There are plenty of people in this neighborhood that I don't associate with. We haven't the right to build a wall around ourselves.

Members of the Emerald Society of New York City parade past St. Patrick's Cathedral on that saint's feast day, a well-known ethnic celebration that extends beyond the Irish-American community. Courtesy Wide World Photos.

Ethnicity as Expressed in Organizational Life

Try as they will, immigrants lose their battle to hold onto the ways of their mother countries. The sons and daughters (second generation) of the newcomers direct their attention to American events and standards, American language, dress, recreation, work, and literature as the old-world culture fades out. The immigrant group becomes "Americanized" in most of its cultural practices, but the group is not absorbed *socially* into the rest of society. The immigrant minority still maintains a social substructure, a network of formal and informal organizations composed of fellow ethnics.

What are the reasons for this? We have already noted that native-born Americans did not accept the newcomer because such association meant a loss of status. The second generation of immigrants found no big welcome mat either. The social web of associations of old-stock, established groups isolated the minority.

Internal reasons operate also. In addition to common economic interests, common origins, and shared experiences, there is the satisfaction of being with those like oneself. A city can be a lonely, impersonal place; the ethnic group for the migrant to the city serves as a sort of family. The migrant can relax among those who understand him, who think as he does and are struggling with problems similar to his. Often he may even be able to say, "My mother knows your mother."

Those who came to the city with the same kinds of disadvantages created by a different race, different language, a different religion or national origin find comfort and support in creating organizations for their own ethnic group. Ethnic groups set up hospitals, old peoples' homes, banks, charitable organizations, churches, and cultural organizations. These are parallel institutions serving similar needs as those institutions of the larger society, yet separated by ethnic sponsorship and membership. For example, within a few city blocks a Jewish old-age home, Polish old-age home, and an Italian old-age home can be found, each serving its own respective group.

Parallel institutions serve as ethnic indicators. Professor Milton Gordon has written:

> From the cradle in the sectarian hospital to the child's play group, to the social clique in high school, the fraternity and religious center in college, the dating group within which he searches for a spouse, the marriage partner, the neighborhood of residence, the church affiliation and church clubs, the men's and the women's social and service clubs, the adult clique of "married," the vacation resort, and then as the age-cycle nears completion, the rest home for the elderly and finally, the sectarian cemetery—in all these activities and relationships which are close to the core of personality and selfhood—the member of the ethnic group may, if he wishes, and will in fact in many cases, follow a path which never takes him across the boundaries of his ethnic subsocietal network.

Is Gordon's observation correct? Does it apply to people today? It is the purpose of Section 3 to help answer these questions. The first experience presents clippings from newspapers which illustrate the variety of parallel institutions which function in society. Topic 18 shows how parallel institutions came about historically as a reaction of the immigrant generation to its new environment. Two mutual aid societies are examined, organizations founded so that members could pool their money in a kind of insurance policy for a time of need. Materials illustrate how present-day business and unions also may be organized to serve an ethnic group. A news story about the grape fields of California attest to that generalization. Churches themselves are parallel institutions catering to the religious needs of various denominations. Topic 19 explores the rise of the national parish or ethnic church, a sort of parallel institution within a parallel institution, catering to a national origins group within the three large religious bodies: Catholic, Protestant, and

Jewish. Topic 20 introduces you to ethnic newspapers where the news is tailored to the interests of one social community.

All of the above topics illustrate the theme that ethnic organizations meet the needs of its members. Topic 21 employs research suggested in an earlier topic and asks you to analyze and interpret it against a model designed by a sociologist who examined what parallel institutions have done for America's Polish community.

Topics 22 and 23 demonstrate the theme that important and persistant public issues grow out of both formal and informal ethnic institutions. Topic 22 raises the question of when may a private organization legally exclude people on the basis of ethnic considerations. Topic 23 speaks of the many people in government and political life who are concerned with the exclusion of large blocs of minorities from educational and economic activity. It examines affirmative action plans and goals to get minorities and women into schools and jobs through preferential treatment, even quotas.

When you have completed the learning experiences in this section, you should be better able to evaluate Milton Gordon's theory about the nature of group life in American society.

Ethnic Organizations Meet the Needs of Their Members

Businessmen from immigrant groups formed banks and savings and loan associations that still may serve their communities. Why do you think they were formed?

What Are Ethnic Parallel Institutions?

Almost all of an individual's decisions are made with a consideration of the groups to which a person consciously or unconsciously belongs. To name a few, a person belongs to a family group, an occupational group, an income-status group (social class: upper, middle, lower), and a friendship group. We have noted how ethnic group membership can be defined by race (white, black, yellow, and such), by religion (Catholic, Protestant, Jewish, and others), by national origin (Swedish-American, German-American, and so on), and by combinations of the above such as white, Anglo-Saxon Protestant. Those groups which an individual uses to help in decision-making are called *reference* groups. Ethnic reference groups, like the other groups, provide the basis for many important personal decisions. Institutions are created to aid in carrying out these decisions. Those quoted in the news items that follow grew out of choices employing the ethnic factor in individuals' business, social, cultural, educational, and recreational life.

As you examine the following adapted news items, try to determine 1) *What are parallel institutions?* 2) *What do they do for their members?* Included at the end of this learning experience are guidelines for examining such organizations. You might want to examine an ethnic parallel institution, perhaps one to which you belong.

The various news items on the following pages of this topic are reprinted with permission from the *Philadelphia Evening Bulletin* and the *Philadelphia Inquirer,* except items 0 through R are fictional.

111

A.
Councilman Zazyczny Gives
Colleagues a Polish Lesson

"I am happy to learn that the emphasis at this convention will be to make Polish-American youth aware of their heritage," City Councilman Joseph Zazyczny said at the opening of the convention of the Polish National Union of America. The Polish Union, a fraternal insurance organization, was founded by bishops of the Polish National Catholic Church, established by dissident Polish Roman Catholics who broke away from the original church organization because they felt American Catholic church officials discriminated against Polish immigrants.

State Rep. Pezak stated, "We still have an obligation to Poland where our loved ones, we pray, will walk in freedom."

B.
Gratz College Schedules Its 71st
Graduation Exercise

Eighteen students will receive Bachelor of Hebrew Literature Degrees. Ninety-two students of Gratz College high-school department, representing the largest graduating class in the department's history, will receive diplomas.

C.
Catholic Students Face Higher
Tuition

Costs rising faster than income may force a $70 increase in registration fee for pupils attending the thirty-one diocesan Roman Catholic high schools.

D.   **NAACP Asks D.A. to Probe Police Killings**

Officials of the National Association for the Advancement of Colored People (NAACP) called Tuesday for an investigation of Monday night's two fatal shootings by policemen. NAACP asserted lesser force could have been used to make arrests.

E.

The words "Mafia" and "Cosa Nostra" will not be heard on the American Broadcasting Company's television series "The F.B.I." when that program begins its new season in September, the Italian-American Civil Rights League said yesterday.

F.   **Events of Week**

Wlodzimiez Aleksandruk, a young Polish violinist, and Jerome Ossowski, a Temple University music student, will perform during the third annual Young Artist Concert sponsored by the Polish Heritage Society of Philadelphia at 2 P.M. Sunday in the lecture hall of Holy Family College. Pulaski Day Essay Contest winners will be honored.

G.

Harvey Lantz, a singer, will entertain members of the Beth Emeth Congregation with Yiddish and other songs after this year's quarterly congregation meeting at 8 P.M. Sunday.

Chicago's Polish-Americans celebrating the Polish Millenium in Soldiers Field. Courtesy Wide World Photos.

H.   DAR Group to Present Christmas Program

The Daughters of the American Revolution will have a Christmas program at the meeting tomorrow at the home of Mrs. William W. Remmey, Frost Lane, Newtown. The program will be presented by the Washington Crossing Society, Children of the American Revolution.

I.   Events of Week

The Federation of United Irish-American Societies will honor Frank E. Burke as "man of the year" at a testimonial dinner-dance Sunday at the Irish Center, Carpenter Lane and Emlen Street, Germantown.

J.   Soccer

Ukranian Nationals vs. United German-Hungarians in District United States, open cup final, tomorrow at 2 P.M. at Edison Field, 29th and Cambria streets.

K. **Future Dim for Hospital in West Philadelphia**

Mercy-Douglas Owes $612,000
Credit Is Cut Off
by John F. Clancy

Mercy Douglas Hospital, one of the city's oldest black institutions, may be forced to close because of mounting debts, including more than $612,000 owed to the Federal Government in payroll deductions.

L. **Mr. Sullivan Tackles Poverty**

The Reverend Leon M. Sullivan, pastor of the Zion Baptist Church, board member of the General Motors Corporation, richly deserves the highest award of the NAACP, the Spingarn Medal, which he received in Minneapolis.

He has been an articulate and effective spokesman for "learn, baby, learn and earn, baby, earn" as the way for minority groups to help themselves out of poverty. His Opportunities Industrialization Center (OIC) has been an inspiring American success story.

It has been reported that OIC now has $25 million to work with. The Rev. Mr. Sullivan estimates that it should have at least $100 million to do the job it has set out to do, and he is critical of the Federal Government for not supplying more of it.

Few of his fellow citizens will challenge the Rev. Mr. Sullivan's belief, however, that "the black man must never permit himself to get into the position of having to depend on the government to sustain and support him all his years .... As long as the government supports a man, the government will be able to control a man and even destroy a man .... As long as our people have to crawl and beg for a few crumbs from the table, so long will our people be pushed around and kicked around and treated like second-class citizens.''

That goes for more than just black people or any other minority people; it goes for all who can't make it to a self-sustaining level, currently estimated at one in eight among us.

We have long admired the work of the Rev. Mr. Sullivan and the OIC; we hope they get every chance to expand and improve their program. Self-reliance may be an old-fashioned virtue, but it hasn't been topped as an essential for independence by any other.

> Editorial of July 10, 1971; reprinted by permission of the *Philadelphia Inquirer*.

M.   **Ruth Seltzer, The Philadelphia Story**
Report on Society

Wednesday evening, Mr. and Mrs. Walter M. Jeffords, Jr., jetted home from Europe. On Thursday, they gave a dinner for 130 guests at the Radnor Hunt Club. The dinner was on the eve of the 51st annual Bryn Mawr Hound Show. Everywhere we saw another master of foxhounds or master of beagles.

Mr. Jeffords is joint master of Mr. Jeffords' Andrews Bridge Hounds. Comasters with him are Robert H. Crompton III and Bob's brother-in-law, George Strawbridge, Jr.

N.   **Organizations**

An outdoor "Star of David Meditation Center" will be dedicated at 2:30 P.M. Sunday in Shalom Memorial Park at Pine and Byberry roads.

O.   **Miss Dugan Engaged to Thomas McGown**

Miss Dugan, who was graduated from the Convent of the Sacred Heart, of Bloomfield Hills, Michigan, and St. Mary's College, Notre Dame, Indiana, is in her third year of Medical School at the College of Medicine of the University of Michigan. She was a debutante of the 1965 season. Her father is vice-president and treasurer of the Chrysler Corporation.

Mr. McGown was graduated from St. Joseph's College and received his Ph.D. degree at University of Notre Dame.

P.   **Elaine Madison Wed to Bradford F. Franklin**

Miss Elaine Madison, daughter of Mr. and Mrs. Nicholas Madison, Jr., of Penn Valley, became the bride of Mr. Bradford Flint Franklin of New York, Saturday at St. Matthew's Episcopal Church. The Rev. J. Edgar Talbot and the Rev. H. Morton Franklin officiated at the five o'clock ceremony.

Miss Madison's grandparents are Brig. General James Madison III of Melmar, Bethayres, and the late Mrs. Sarah Lippincott Madison and Mr. and Mrs. Richard Olney of Bryn Mawr.

Mr. Franklin is an alumnus of Groton School, Harvard College and the University of Pennsylvania Law School. His grandparents are Mrs. Reginald L. Franklin of Troy, New York, and the late Mr. and Mrs. C. Morton Franklin of Binghamton, New York.

Q.   **Harry Jesse Dies: Law Firm Partner**

Harry Jesse, a partner in the law firm of Blaustein, Jesse, and Wolfman, died Wednesday at the

Temple University Hospital. Fifty-two years of age, he resided at 1613 Saturn Road, Elkins Park.

He was a member of the American, Pennsylvania, and Philadelphia Bar Associations and the Tax Section of the Philadelphia Bar. He lectured at the New York University Tax Institute, the Tax Institute of C.P.A.'s tax forums. He served as past president of the Young Men's and Young Women's Hebrew Association, as a trustee of the Federation of Jewish Agencies' Endowment Program and served on the boards of directors of the Federation of Jewish Charities and the Federation of Jewish Charities Foundation, Temple Sinai, and Ashbourne Country Club.

An Army veteran, he co-authored two books on taxes. Jesse was the only son of the late Rabbi Jesse and the late Bessie Serebrier Jesse.

His wife, the former Bertha Isaacman, his son, and two sisters survive him.

Services will be held at Levine's and internment will be held in Har Zion Cemetery.

R.   **Francis J. Grobowski, Kensington Lawyer**

Francis J. Grobowski, 61, died Wednesday at his home at 8900 E. Allegheny Avenue, where he also maintained his law office.

Mr. Grobowski graduated from Temple University Law School, receiving a doctor of law degree.

He served as director and legal counsel of the First Center City Savings and Loan Association of Philadelphia. He participated as a member of the Polish Army Veterans, the Polish National Alliance, the Polish Beneficial Association and the Polish-American Association.

Mr. Grobowski, a past chairman of the Pulaski Day Celebration, helped sponsor that event

A funeral can be an occasion for ethnic groups and organizations to honor the memory of one of their own members.

associated with the Polish-American Congress of Eastern Pennsylvania.

His wife, the former Josephine Pisack, and two brothers survive him.

Requiem Mass will be celebrated at 9:30 A.M. Thursday at St. Adalbert's Roman Catholic Church, E. Allegheny Avenue and Thompson Street.

GUIDELINES FOR EXAMINING A PARALLEL INSTITUTION

1. Find out how the organization began.
2. Give some background on why and how the group got its name.
3. Give some background on the parent group (if the organization is a chapter or affiliated with a larger organization).
4. Tell what purposes the organization served when it first began.
5. Describe briefly the organization and quote from the early constitution or charter.
6. Tell what kind of people made up the early membership.
7. Tell who the membership consists of today.
8. Describe the nature and activities of the organization today.

9. Go to a meeting and give a detailed description of what happened there.
10. Interview some members and officers of the organization; quote from and summarize their comments on the activities and the advantages of belonging to the organization.
11. Provide details of any one activity or project carried on by the organization.
12. Attach some literature put out by the group and analyze the content according to what it provides for the group (ideology, pool of associates, etc.)
13. Comment on where you think the group is heading today—gaining strength, weakening, holding fast to members. Explain.

General Comments

The parallel institution you examine may be one you belong to or one with which your parents, relatives, or friends are associated. It may be an ethnic, church, charitable, welfare, cultural, educational, defense, or social organization. All sources you use should be identified; interviews should include the person's name, the date, and the place where interview took place. You may add footnote references or include a bibliography of sources of information gathered.

Why Do Self-Help Ethnic Organizations Form?

Uprooted from familiar surroundings, the immigrants came upon an America that gave little assistance to the sick and widowed poor. Today Social Security provides some help for these people. The first two selections that follow contain adapted versions of constitutions of ethnic organizations. Note the timing and kind of benefits offered. These two organizations still exist despite the presence today of many insurance plans, both private and governmental. Can you figure out why?

The third selection, "La Causa," is an account of the formation of the United Farm Workers, a union organized along ethnic lines, a self-help institution for Mexican Americans established in the 1960s. It illustrates that parallel institutions can be found in the world of business and labor as well as in the social world.

As you read these selections, try to determine what each of these organizations do for their members. Read "in between the lines" and determine what they are doing that is not directly stated. *Be ready to identify the phrases upon which you base your answers.* Compare the three organizations and list at least three aspects they have in common. Consider reasons for establishing these ethnic organizations, how they serve to unite the ethnic group, and how they reflect the values and concerns of their respective membership.

CONSTITUTION AND BYLAWS OF THE INDEPENDENT YOUNG
MEN'S BENEFICIAL ASSOCIATION ORGANIZED IN
PHILADELPHIA IN 1910

Article I.   Title and Language
Sec. 1.   This association shall be known by the name of Independent Young Men's Beneficial Association. This name shall not be changed as long as seven (7) members in good standing remain to support it.
Sec. 2.   All the business of the Association shall be conducted in Yiddish or English.
Sec. 3.   Correspondence may be carried on in Yiddish or English.

Article II.   Object
Sec. 1.   The object and purpose of the Association shall be to promote good fellowship and brotherly love among its members, to aid its members in case of sickness or distress, and to provide for their burial and death benefits.

Article IV.   Membership
Any man of the Jewish faith who is physically sound and of good moral character, between the ages of 18 and 35, and, if married, is lawfully married to a Jewish woman may be proposed as a member of this Association.

Article V.   Benefits
Sec. 8.   No sickness benefit shall be paid to any member when the sickness was caused by immorality.
Sec. 9.   The officers shall appoint a social visiting committee of three to visit every sick member whether he is entitled to a sickness benefit or not.

Article VI.   Deaths
Sec. 1.   When a member in good standing dies, or his registered wife dies, the Association shall provide a burial dress, a plain coffin, a hearse, two automobiles—one for the officers of the Association and one for the immediate family—watchman service for one night and burial ground.
Sec. 6.   At the death of a member or of his wife who is registered with the Association the members shall be notified by mail or a notice shall be inserted in a Jewish newspaper.
Sec. 7.   Upon the death of a member the surviving spouse shall

receive a sum of $500. This endowment shall be obtained by an assessment of 75¢ per member per month.

An Old-Age Fund set aside from funds collected shall pay the dues of those who have reached 65 years of age and are unable to derive any income.

CONSTITUTION OF THE POLISH BENEFICIAL ASSOCIATION FOUNDED 1899, BRIDESBURG SECTION, PHILADELPHIA, PENNSYLVANIA

Article I. Name

The name of the corporation is The Polish Beneficial Association; in Polish, Poliskie Stewarzyszenie Kasy pod Opieka Jana Nantego Stanach Zjednoczonych.

Article II. Scope and Purpose

The purpose of this Association is the organization of Polish men and women and of others of Slavic descent of the Roman or Greek Catholic faith residing in Pennsylvania or other states where this Corporation has been chartered, for their insurance in the event of death, as well as aiding members of their families in cases of permanent bodily disability or sickness.

The Association will collect dues and other payment from members to assure the payment of benefits to members and their widows and families.

The Association will support Polish knowledge and culture by maintaining a newspaper and by printing and distributing other suitable writings.

The Association will aid Polish charitable institutions.

Article III. Membership

A member of this Association may be any person of good moral reputation of Polish, Lithuanian, or Slavic descent of the Roman or Greek Catholic faith.

Persons not of Polish, Lithuanian, or Slavic descent who are related by marriage to a Polish or Slavic person and who are of the Roman or Greek Catholic faith may become members of this Association.

Charges and Benefits in 1899

A $1.00 assessment per month is made for the death insurance benefits. A 5¢ assessment is added for clerical handling, and a 50¢ per month assessment is added for membership in the Central Polish Organization.

At the death of a male member in good standing the widow shall receive $600; should a wife die, the husband shall receive $300.

Young Lords Occupy Church, Plan Center for Drug Addicts

by Sam Ettinger and Dominic Sama

A group of young Puerto Rican militants—aged 10 to 18— took over a North Philadelphia church Friday and announced plans to convert it into a center to help drug addicts and put pushers out of business.

The pastor of the King's Way Community Lutheran Church in America, 1720 Mount Vernon st., consented to the take-over after the building was seized by the Young Lords, the Puerto Rican counterpart to the Black Panthers.

Wilfredo Rojas, the Lords' 18-year-old lieutenant of education, said the plan to help drug addicts would go into effect Sunday morning. Meanwhile, "revolutionary" religious services would be provided for the church's active members, mostly Puerto Ricans, Rojas said.

While young children sang and danced in a section of the church, Rojas told a press conference the Lords would

_____Establish communications through underground contacts with pushers in the area in a bid to stop the drug traffic. "We are not a violent group and we want to keep it that way," Rojas said. "But if the pushers do not cooperate, then we will seek their

Reprinted by permission of the *Philadelphia Inquirer*, November 7, 1970.

Young Lords demonstrating their solidarity.
Courtesy *Philadelphia Inquirer*/Michael Viola.

cooperation through other means,'' he said. He did not elaborate on ''other means.''

_____Keep the church open around the clock beginning Sunday, after which hot breakfasts would be available for needy children and adults in the neighborhood.

_____Provide legal aid service at all hours for addicts and arrested pushers who cooperate.

_____Maintain an all-night medical station in the church for addicts who seek comfort and aid.

Rojas did not mention how funds would be raised to finance the Lords' campaign against drugs.

The Rev. Roger Zepernick, 28, pastor of the church, said he has worked with the Young Lords in various community projects and agreed with the take-over.

''The occupation of this building is in the tradition of the church,'' Rev. Zepernick said. ''I believe the community itself should take the forefront in solving community problems.''

He said the Lords' occupation of his church might ''control the pushers and violence that has been going on in this area.''

The church is near 17th and Wallace sts., the scene of drug raids and arrests by police this week.

Rev. Zepernick said his congregation boasts about 50 active members, mostly Puerto Ricans.

The church, sparsely furnished and badly in need of painting and repair, was erected in 1874. It has housed various religious denominations and often served as a community center.

Earlier in the day, Juan Ramos, 19, captain of the Young Lords' chapter here, accused the "white establishment" of inducing barrio residents to become drug addicts and pushers.

"Our people don't grow poppies in our backyards; they have only rats there," Ramos told a rally of 75 persons at 17th and Wallace sts. "We don't go to Turkey to get the dope," he said. "Our people aren't born junkies; they're made junkies. They aren't born with syringes in their hands; the needles are put there by the white establishment."

The rally began as a parade at 1720 Mount Vernon st. and wound through the Spanish speaking community until it ended at 17th and Wallace sts.

La Causa

Many Mexicans became Americans when a large area of Mexico was annexed to the United States after the American victory in the 1848 Mexican-American War. Many more Mexicans have flocked across the U.S.-Mexico border since then, particularly in the past thirty years, to find a better life. 4,617,000 Americans with Spanish last names live in the Southwestern states—California, Arizona, Colorado, New Mexico, and Texas. These Mexican Americans are a people descended from the early Spanish settlers and the native Indians.

Probably the most well-known Chicano (as Mexican Americans are often called) is César Chávez, organizer of migrant workers in the Southwest. He has organized strikes among field hands

Story written especially for students by the author.

César Chávez leads his United Farm Workers in picketing a Seattle, Washington, supermarket. What could he hope to gain through such actions? Courtesy Wide World Photos.

for higher wages and better working conditions and he has acquired many members for his union, the United Farm Workers. The farm-labor movement, the grape strike of the early 1970s, and activities for the advancement of Mexican Americans in general are known as *La Causa*.

Chávez came to *La Causa* from long experience with the problems of Chicanos. Born in the United States, he has known poverty, backbreaking field labor, and especially discrimination. As a dark-haired, dark-skinned sensitive boy he felt the sting of the last in barbershops, in theaters, in restaurants, and, most important, in jobs. In a seamy *barrio* (the Mexican-American quarter of San Jose, California), César as a young man joined the Community Service Organization, an activist group, the brainchild of Saul Alinsky. Alinsky developed the technique of helping communities of poor people gain economic and political power by uniting and using boycotts, demonstrations, and picketing, as well as bloc (group) voting, to gain better conditions. César worked for ten years learning how to organize fellow Chicanos. In 1962 he set out to do something about the poor pay, bad working conditions, and unhealthy living accommodations of farm workers.

Chávez took all the money he had, a mere $1,200 in savings, and began the National Farm Workers Association in the San Joaquin Valley town of Delano. With this as a base, he drove his 1953 Mercury station wagon over 300,000 miles throughout the valley as he talked to more than 50,000 workers.

Like European immigrants who came decades ago, Chávez found Chicanos attracted to death-plan benefits, cheap burial plots, and a credit union which offered low-rate loans to needy members. To keep recruits informed, a union newspaper, *El Malcriado* (The Misfit), circulated among 18,000 families. But the main task of a union is to improve working conditions.

The National Farm Workers Association won its first victory when it took an employer to court for paying less than the federal minimum wage. When the case was won, Mexican-American migrants saw that it was possible to "beat the boss." Flushed with success, the tiny union sued over poor housing conditions in two farm-labor camps. Farm workers live quite near the fields where they work. In Tulare County, California, accommodations were 9-by-11-foot tin shacks with no toilets or other plumbing. Workers boiled in the summer and froze in the winter. When Tulare County responded by ordering modern accommodations, Chávez gained new union members.

Back in Delano the grape growers hired Filipino field hands and Mexicans who came across the Rio Grande border. They paid the latter more wages, so the Filipinos, who were organized in a group called the Agricultural Workers Organizing Committee, went on strike for equal pay. Chávez, in an exuberant meeting in a Roman Catholic Church, urged the Filipinos to join him to form the United Farm Workers, and a big strike was called against the grape growers. The strike became a cause for uniting field hands in Chávez's union and getting the growers to recognize the union's right to sit down and bargain for better wages and working conditions.

Many of the grape growers were of Yugoslavian and Italian extraction who had come to the San Joaquin Valley during the first four decades of the twentieth century. They had little but the shirts on their backs; however, from southern Europe they knew the art of growing grapes. By hard work and diligent saving they bought farms and built them into fair-sized family enterprises. Costs of raising grapes soared in the 1960s, while the prices of grapes, and hence profits, did not rise. Growers felt hard pressed to raise wages.

The long strike became a nationwide boycott, with sympathetic housewives refusing to buy California-grown grapes. Many groups, aided by Chávez's personal appearances, were able to publicize the grape pickers' cause and the sale of grapes declined. Faced by a loss of business and disruption of production, a contract was signed with the United Farm Workers.

Currently Chavez has moved into organizing lettuce pickers. *La Causa,* with its flag of a black Aztec eagle in a red field with images of the Mexican version of Mary, the Virgin of Guadalupe, faces a tough fight with both growers and a rival union. Chávez believes that his organization can do the most to improve the lives of Mexican-American field hands and in that way help the entire Chicano community.

What Does a National Church Do for Its Members?

We may say that all churches are already "ethnic" in the sense that members have a sense of togetherness, a group consciousness based on religious background, and that sponsorship and membership consists of those with the same religious persuasion. However, even within large denominations some churches seem to be set aside for those having the same national origin. The Roman Catholics call such churches "national churches." For example, worshippers of Polish descent may join a Polish national church, Italians attend an Italian national church, and so on. Most Roman Catholic churches serve geographic areas, and Catholics of all national origins join them.

This lesson contains an interview with an Italian-American priest about the formation and activities of an Italian national church in a large city. It is accompanied by photos which help illustrate the speaker's remarks. *As you read the interview, list the ways this church meets the needs of its parishioners. Do you agree with the pastor that the longevity of this church is due mainly to the continuing immigration of Italians?*

After you have read the interview, read the newspaper article that follows. To what extent are the requests outlined in the article similar or dissimilar to the services the Italian national church offers its parishioners?

Our Lady of Loreto Catholic Church and School.

TRANSCRIPT OF INTERVIEW WITH PASTOR OF AN ITALIAN NATIONAL CHURCH

Interviewer:

Father I. E. Schifalacqua is the spiritual head of Our Lady of Loreto Catholic Church and School, an Italian national parish in Philadelphia.

Interviewer:

Father Schifalacqua, why is this church called Our Lady of Loreto?

Father S.:

In honor of the Blessed Virgin Mother. She has many titles in many countries. Tradition tells us that a house mysteriously appeared intact in Loreto, Italy, transported, we don't know how, from Nazareth, Palestine, under the influence of the Holy Mother. Since Italian immigrants founded this church here, they chose an Italian way of honoring the Virgin by naming this church after that event.

Interviewer:

What can you tell us about the founding of this church and the founding of other Italian-oriented churches?

Father S.:

The main reason for the so-called Italian national parishes was the language barrier. Those who came over from Italy could only speak Italian. If they went to the established parishes in America, they would not understand what was going on. In order to preserve their faith, the immigrants asked for priests who could understand their language.

As Italians moved out from the original settlement and as new immigrants settled in other parts of the city, additional Italian national parishes grew up. Italians in this neighborhood petitioned Cardinal Dougherty, then head of Roman Catholic affairs in Philadelphia, for their own priest and their own church geared to the needs of Italian immigrants—a national church. In September 1932 the Cardinal assigned Father Amateis, who had trained in Italy purposely to aid Italian immigrants in America, to this area with the mission of establishing a church. Once built, the church served the immigrant generation and its descendants.

The Roman Catholic Church saw the national parish as a stop-gap measure. Its object was, and still is, to see an end to the national church as Italians become more Americanized, as they master the English language. Then Italians along with other Catholics would attend a territorial parish. The national church did not vanish, for immigration from Italy has not stopped; the immigrant goes to a place where the language is familiar.

Interviewer:

Who makes up your membership today?

Father S.:

Mainly parishioners of Italian extraction. The students at the parochial school are largely of Italian descent, although many are products of intermarriage. The segregation that once existed be-

If a particular town in Italy had a procession in honor of a certain saint, that custom was carried over by members of that town here in America.

tween the Irish and the Italians is breaking down. If one of the parents has an Italian background, the child may attend our school. Both parents must join our church. Those with a non-Italian background attend the territorial parish.

Interviewer:

What religious observances of this church are particularly Italian?

Father S.:

If a particular town in Italy had a procession in honor of a particular saint, that custom was carried over by members of that town here in America. Many in this neighborhood came from a region outside Naples. At first a small group came; then they wrote back encouraging others to come. Those who followed gravitated toward the neighborhood where their fellow townsmen lived. In Italy they took out the statues of the saints Our Lady of Mount Carmel and St. Anthony and formed a procession behind them. We do that here. We have a celebration for a few days, a carnival with booths, fireworks, and music, climaxed by a procession.

We used to celebrate Mass in both Italian and English. Then the Italian Mass was held Sunday mornings at 8 A.M. Attendance at this Mass dropped, for the congregants knew English. Now we have the Italian Mass only on the first Sunday of each month. The Mass we celebrate now is standard in all Roman Catholic churches. Sometimes congregants both young and old like the strumming of a guitar, so we have that often now.

Interviewer:

What societies are attached to the church and what do they do?

Father S.:

We have the Sacred Heart Society for the women. It is commonly known as the "Mothers' Club."

The Holy Name Society is for men. The purpose of these organizations is spiritual—to get people to services, to become interested in religious activities. The only time they become materialistic is when they engage in fund-raising activities.

Interviewer:

What do you see in the future of Our Lady of Loreto? Will its members gradually drift away?

Father S.:

In this section of the city the church is overcrowded; membership has increased as more parents are sending their children to parochial school rather than public school. But in other areas of the city Italian national churches are closing. When the Italians move away, their church closes and another one is not opened up at another place. The Italians disperse to other neighborhoods and join the territorial parish where Catholics of all backgrounds attend.

Black Catholics Urge Cardinal to Respond to Their Needs

by **Andrew Wallace**
Inquirer Religion Writer

The Black Lay Catholic Caucus urged John Cardinal Krol on Thursday to give his personal attention to the needs of black Catholics in the city.

The black group, which now has 200 adherents throughout the city, according to Hammock [spokesman for caucus], is one of hundreds of such groups forming around the country in connection with the NOBC.

It was formed in August, and on Sept. 29, delivered a paper outlining its goals and setting forth 18 "demands" to the archdiocese.

The demands called for more black priests and sisters, development of a black liturgy, black studies at the seminary, and elimination of the "missionary mentality" of white priests and sisters assigned to black areas.

Other demands were for parish councils in black parishes to be given a say in all decisions, development of programs for youth and black awareness and for "meaningful sermons" relevant to blacks as a race.

On schools, major requests were for black administrators, emphasis on black studies and open admissions for all black Catholics.

The caucus' primary goals concerned schools, parish councils, recruiting of black priests and endorsement and funding NOBC, Hammock said.

Reprinted by permission of the *Philadelphia Inquirer*, November 13, 1970.

What Does an Ethnic Newspaper Tell?

Many American ethnic newspapers began as foreign-language newspapers providing immigrants with news in a language they could understand. Dominated at first by news from the "mother country," in a short time they switched the emphasis to news about the affairs of new Americans and American events that affected the newcomers. As the old folks died and immigration dwindled after 1924, some of the papers faded out, while others switched to English. Other journals, published weekly or monthly and covering large geographic areas, printed news about the ethnic group not available in the general press.

In this lesson you will read an English-language weekly of a Middle Eastern ethnic group, the Armenians, and a newspaper published for the black community in Philadelphia. The Armenian paper is only a few years old and was founded to serve second- and third-generation Armenian Americans, most of whom cannot read Armenian. In 1976 the *Philadelphia Tribune* celebrated its ninetieth birthday, to make it the oldest continuously published black newspaper in the world. About the time of World War I the editor and publisher, Cris Perry, saw in the arrival of thousands of black migrants from Virginia and North Carolina to work in Philadelphia's defense industries a golden opportunity for the newspaper to raise circulation and advertising revenue. He placed in the paper news about the newcomers' former homes in the South and news about the newcomers' activities in the city. The plan worked. Circulation rose both in Philadelphia and in the near South.

As you read the excerpts that follow, first determine the nature and purpose of each article and who is likely to take an interest in it. Then list at least four ways in which the two papers are alike and one major way the papers differ.

136

Editorials and Comment

The TRIBUNE'S Policy Will Not Be Altered

The policy of the *Philadelphia Tribune,* initiated forty-eight years ago by E. Washington Rhodes, will not be altered to any basic extent under the leadership of those upon whose shoulders now falls the responsibility for the newspaper's policy and publication.

It might be well at this time to document for the reminder of those who know, and for the information of those who don't, that the *Tribune*'s policy has been to secure for the Black population all the rights and privileges guaranteed to any citizen under the Constitution of the United States, the laws of the Commonwealth of Pennsylvania, and the ordinances of the City of Philadelphia.

As a reminder to those who know and for the information of those who don't, it might be well to relate, if not in the order of their happening, some of the movements brought to a successful fruition under the leadership or with the support of the *Philadelphia Tribune.*

We wonder how many Black public school teachers now teaching in senior and junior high schools know that the fight to get a Negro teacher in a junior high school had the support of the *Tribune.* Today's teachers take it for granted. Yesterday's teachers were barred.

Most of today's teachers teaching in schools with white children ought to be reminded of the time when there were TWO lists for teachers, and one of those lists was used for the appointment and promotion of Black teachers to Black schools only. The *Tribune*'s fight on the dual list brought the change.

The political story is an interesting one. A Black politician in the 30th Ward suggested to the then leader of the Republican party in Philadelphia that the time had come to have a Black magistrate and other political recognition for Blacks. The haughty reply was, "I don't have to worry about Negroes; I have their votes in my vest pocket."

The *Tribune* took up the challenge. We campaigned for a Negro magistrate, and Amos Scott was chosen.

That accomplished, the *Tribune* began to use at the end of each news story the endline "A Negro Councilman," and the late James H. Irvin, widely known businessman and churchman, was elected.

Our next headline advocated "A Negro Judge." This campaign was not easily won, but it was. The late Herbert E. Millen was appointed judge of a Court of Record by the late Governor Duff at a public meeting conducted under *Tribune* auspices at Convention Hall.

[The editorial goes on to tell about other campaigns for political posts.]

Over the years we have joined with "fighters" like the late John K. Rice in community advancement. There had been campaigns, believe it or not, for the use of police "red cars" by Black policemen, the promotion of Black policemen beyond the patrolman rank, the use of Black policemen to direct traffic, and the promotion of Black firemen—in all these advances the *Tribune* played a leading part. The truth is that the *Philadelphia Tribune,* under the farsighted leadership of Mr. Rhodes, has been the instrument through which slowly but surely the Black man has been able to secure rights and privileges in this city and elsewhere hitherto denied to him.

Adapted from the *Philadelphia Tribune,* June 10, 1970

How might the content of *The Philadelphia Tribune* for
blacks differ from the general press?

A. *Philadelphia Tribune*

The Family Assistance Plan Called "Racist, Dehumanizing"

Mrs. Roxanne Jones has charged this bill
harasses the poor and is a giant step backward. The
poor would have to accept jobs even if they paid
$1.20 an hour.

Housing Bill Is Called Dangerous

All eyes of persons interested in full and equal
housing in Pennsylvania are now focused on
Pennsylvania House Bill 959. It states that any pro-
posal to build public housing would require the approval of the residents of the community where the
housing is to be built.

Highest Physical Educational
Award Is Won by Teacher

By James Cassell

Mrs. Ophelia C. Little, a teacher at the George Washington Carver Elementary School for twenty-one years, became the first black to receive the William H. Stecher Award, presented by Robert L. Poindexter, executive deputy superintendent of the public school system.

Don Newcombe Relives Athletic
Feats As He Views 'The Black
Athlete'

The Black Athlete is a film that traces the history of the black man in sports.

Mr. Help

Mr. W. E. B. of 1300 block of East Cliveden Street writes, "I am going to move this summer from the city to the suburbs. I am writing to see if there is an organization that helps people making such a move."

MR. HELP suggests you contact Suburban Fair Housing Inc., Ardmore, Pennsylvania. Miss Margaret Collins of this organization has helped others in your position.

Fire Captain's Wife Mourned

Funeral services for the young wife of Captain Roland C. Lewis will be held today. Her husband is president of Club Valiants, the organization of black fire fighters.

Book Published about OIC

Lawrence D. Reddick, professor of history at Temple University, traces the history and outlines the successful educational and training methods of the Opportunities Industrialization Center.

Tribune Presents Album of June Graduates

Carol Platter of East Mt. Airy has graduated from Immaculate College, where she was consistently named to the Dean's List and listed in Who's Who Among Students. Her B.A. is in history.

Capital Punishment Alive and Kicking

by Ronald H. Brown
Associate Director
National Urban League

The death penalty ought to be abolished either by a future court ruling or by legislative action. It fails as a deterrent to crime and it is applied in a discriminatory manner. In the past 40 years almost 4,000 people have been executed in the United States. The majority, 55%, have been blacks.

Comments from Tribune Readers

To the Editor:

Concerning gang activity in Philadelphia. It is something that goes way back, including faculty-parent-child relations, early psychological traumas, and undesirable social conditions. A predisposing factor is a neglected childhood. The neglected child feels he is missing something....

David Taylor

Progress in Business and
Government Areas

(EDITORS' NOTE: This series of profiles deals with what Negroes are doing in the government and business fields. The accomplishments of the men and women featured should inspire others to higher achievements despite handicaps by the score.)

Community Calendar

June 12—A drawing will be held by Mom's Crippens' Community Center, 1240 W. Girard, on behalf of Better Play Street.

Afro-American Auto Association

We do not front for anybody: We are not only black owned and operated, but we refuse to sell to anyone who discriminates against black people.

The above news items are adapted from the *Philadelphia Tribune,* June 12, 1971.

B. *The Armenian Reporter*

Editorial

Survival or Freedom

Since the establishment of Soviet power in Armenia after the short-lived independent Republic of the Dashnay Party, a favorite subject of discussion has been the issue of freedom for Armenia— whether Armenia under the present Soviet system enjoys the benefits of a free country or if it is under

Newspapers from all nations bring news from the Old World to American ethnic communities. Courtesy the Library of Congress.

some sort of oppression from a strange and foreign ruler.

In the Armenian Dispersion where a number of political parties have existed—all of them founded prior to the establishment of Soviet Armenia—there have been three independent views regarding this matter. One of them is the view that Armenia is totally subjugated by the Soviet Union and does not enjoy freedom as an independent country, and therefore the prime concern of the Armenians in the diaspora (lands in which Armenians live outside Armenia) should be the liberation of the land from the system under which it presently exists.

The second and more moderate view with a large following is that of accepting present-day Armenia the way it is, although not approving of the communist system which has been in existence in that country, accepting it as sort of a price for enjoying freedom from the more oppressive tyranny of the centuries-old enemies that have surrounded Armenia.

The third view, forwarded by groups calling themselves progressive, accepts the Soviet system in Armenia as the only one that can give Armenia its present status, and as an ideal form of government.

We believe it is up to the Armenians who live under Soviet rule to change or accept the system, not those outside.

Calendar of Coming Events

Philadelphia, PA., Area

June 13—11th Annual Concert, Knar Armenian Choral Group, St. Joseph's College, 3 P.M.

Hundreds in Watertown Picket Turkish Program Held in Armenian Hall

Watertown, MA. The demonstrators were incensed that Turks had rented an Armenian facility three short weeks after Martyrs' Day marking the 56th anniversary of the Armenian massacres by the Turks.

A Salute to Our Graduates

Post Graduate Work in Armenian Studies Planned by Andres Kzirian of Philadelphia. Philadelphia, PA. Andrew Kzirian was graduated from the College of Education—Temple University with the degree of Bachelor of Science in Education. His area of concentration was social studies with a minor in

Middle Eastern History. This past year he served as National Education Director of the Armenian Youth Federation.

Premiere of Saroyan Play in Yerevan

Yerevan. William Saroyan's play "The Vineyard," written especially for the Armenian stage, was produced by the Sundukyan Drama Theatre in Yerevan.

Book Review
by Susan B. Kelekian

The Bard of Loree, Selected Works of Hovannes Toumanian, compiled and translated by Mischa Kudian, Mashtots Press.

There is an unfortunate lack of solid translations in English of the numerous Armenian authors of the past.

Support the Armenian Sisters Academy Preserve Armenian Future and History

The academy which is a nonpolitical, nonsectarian institution has a governing body of fourteen young members representing the entire Armenian community of five Armenian churches in Philadelphia.

The Connection of Armenian with Modern European Languages

The following is the concluding statement of a lecture by Dr. S. E. Mann, head of the Slavonic studies department at the University of London, and the author of *An Armenian Historical Grammar in Latin Characters*.

Obituaries

Victoria Babaian

Philadelphia, PA. Miss Victoria Babaian, organist of St. Gregory the Illuminator Armenian Church in Philadelphia, passed away at the University of Pennsylvania Hospital at an early age.

Classified

Evergreen Cottages Route 23A
Friendly Homey Atmosphere
R. Ohnigian, Your Host

The above editorial and news items are adapted from the *Armenian Reporter,* June 10, 1971.

GUIDELINES FOR THE INVESTIGATION OF AN ETHNIC NEWSPAPER

1. How do the advertisements reflect the values and customs of the ethnic group?
2. Look at both the classified and general ads. Are there clues in the ads about areas of residence and occupations?
3. Read the editorial page and letters to the editor. What issues trouble the ethnic group?
4. In what ways does the paper relate to the "mother country"?
5. What kind of people are honored? How? For what reasons?
6. What ethnic organizations are promoted in the newspaper?
7. What kinds of news do you find that you would not see in the general press?
8. How does the paper appeal to the various audiences: old, young, intellectual, sports-minded, social-minded, and religious?
9. What proportions of the news are local, national, and foreign?
10. Does the paper favor a particular political position? If so, what is it?

Some general suggestions: Scan more than one issue. When you write up your analysis of the paper, include some clippings to document your remarks.

What Do Parallel Institutions Do for an Ethnic Community?

In previous topics you examined different kinds of ethnic organizations, and you had a close look at some which service members of ethnic groups. Perhaps you had a chance to research one yourself or listen to a classmate give a report of a local parallel institution. At this point you probably have formed some ideas about why these institutions are formed and what they do for the community of members.

With a partner, make a list of what you consider to be the ten most important services (functions) ethnic parallel institutions perform.

You will keep this list and develop a master one with the help of your teacher and the rest of the class. You will test these ideas against what an expert has to say.

The author of the selection that follows describes a Polish community in Chicago which she gives the name "Polonia." She uses the term "community" in a wider sense than we have done so far, so that community is not merely a social group in a neighborhood but includes members of an ethnic group living in the entire greater Chicago area. After living among the people and observing them for three years, she believes that what she says about Polonia applies to other ethnic communities.

Read the following selection. What functions of an ethnic organization does the author list that you mentioned earlier? What functions does she list that you have not already mentioned? To what extent in your view does this author accurately describe the functions of such voluntary associations? What are the reasons for your answer?

What Do Ethnic Organizations Do for an Ethnic Community?

Ethnic voluntary associations develop a series of reasons why they should exist, an ideology. They try to convince members of the ethnic community that it is to their best interest to remain with and work for the subgroup to which they are members. To do this in the case of Polish Americans they try to find those aspects of Polish and Polish-American culture which are common and acceptable to all subgroups of Polonia; then they impart this culture to young and old alike.

They try to answer the questions: What does it mean to be a Polish American? What in our heritage is worth preserving? The associations stress those aspects of the national and Polish-American culture which deal with the literary and artistic achievements, and especially with contributions to world or American culture. Self-confidence and pride are built up by the stress on the superiority of Polish culture.

All ethnic associations have the function of providing members with the companionship of those with a similar background and/or interests. Where participants meet in face-to-face relations, social gatherings are common. Members can relax and feel comfortable with those who share their habits and values. The associations strengthen the "we" feeling and keep marriage and close friendships within Polonia.

"I'd rather be a big fish in here than a nobody out there," said an active association member. Voluntary associations provide members with a chance for prestige. A woman who would be hardly noticed, socially or otherwise, becomes an important figure in a missionary society. A truck driver of average abilities becomes a chairman of a committee. The small neighborhood groups offer such opportunities for ordinary people.

A church is more than a religious institution; it is a community

Adapted from Helena Znaniecki Lopata, "The Function of Voluntary Associations in an Ethnic Community," in Ernest Burgess and Donald Bogue, editors, *Contributions to Urban Sociology* (Chicago: University of Chicago Press, 1964), pp. 203–223.

A Polish beneficial association provides low-cost insurance and other services to members of its community.

center of its own. Its framework is used for social purposes. The immigrant Polish peasant resented leadership from American priests who did not understand his language or his religious ways. Neither he nor the established native American parishioners were comfortable with one another. The Polish immigrants did unite and work hard to build their own churches and parochial schools, old-age homes and orphanages. Social organizations revolved around the church. Today, despite the decreased primary role of religious activities of many groups and the decline of church-related organizations, voluntary associations in Polonia, except for a few, uphold education in and the preservation of Roman Catholicism as one of their functions.

Cheap insurance, particularly life insurance, provides members with an economic motive for their membership. The economic dimension comes out in the professional associations with the prefix "Polish-American." This aids the professional member to gain clients in Polonia. Artists of all types, writers, musicians, and painters of Polish extraction find an audience and a market for their works by the patronage of the ethnic associations. Many organizations need to be staffed, and the positions form a kind of ethnic civil service with a chance of advancement to executive positions. Here again the economic function of the organizations shows.

The occupational groups of professionals mentioned above are a type of special-interest association. So are clubs which bring together persons interested in the same activity—sports and veterans groups, for example. Volunteer associations along ethnic lines meet the needs of these special interests.

The Polish-American press performs many functions which overlap those of the associations. Through the press the Polish-American reader learns about the ideology, the basis of existence of the associations, for the newspapers stress the positive aspects of Polish culture and the importance of identifying with Polish life. It reports the activities of the many ethnic organizations and urges the reader to participate. By reporting news about Polish-Americans who have gained status and have made contributions to the general society, by publicizing activities of leaders and internal conflicts, and by reporting on news items where the larger society has recognized something occurring in Polonia, the reader gets a feeling of the great value and importance of community life.

The political function looms large for these ethnic associations. They act collectively as a large pressure group in trying to influence the policies and actions of the American government by electing or having appointed officials of Polish descent, staging mass protest meetings, writing letters, and other activities. They seek to raise the status of Polonia in the eyes of all Americans. They pressure for inclusion of Polish-American heroes (Kosciuszko, Pulaski) in American history courses in the public schools. They invite the general press and prominent Americans to events where Polish or Polish-American artists perform and guard against evidences of prejudice and discrimination.

Voluntary associations try to define and carry out what the proper relationship should be between the "mother country" and the ethnic community in America. Over the years the Polish community in America has had less and less contact with Poland. In recent times large national organizations, really federations of local organizations throughout the country, have limited their activities to supporting humanitarian efforts such as aid and asylum to Polish refugees and protests of communist government actions in Poland.

Important Public Issues Grow Out of Ethnic Institutions

When May a Private Organization
Legitimately Exclude on an Ethnic Basis?

You have examined various types of private organizations which have set as one of their goals the preservation of an ethnic group. Most people would argue that a club instituted to insure social welfare benefits for Polish immigrants and their descendants or a Jewish temple sisterhood should not be expected to throw open its membership to persons of other faiths and nationalities. But what about private organizations which serve a more general purpose?

The reading selection below tells of a private club organized around recreational activities which has unstated ethnic qualifications for membership. *To what extent do you think such clubs should be able to follow such an exclusionary policy?* After you discuss your views, compose a set of guidelines by which a private organization can be permitted to exclude on an ethnic basis and another list when an organization should not be allowed to discriminate on an ethnic basis.

After you have prepared your sets of guidelines, you will be given a handout containing some excerpts from a Pennsylvania court decision which also sets some guidelines. *Compare your list and the court's decision to see where you and the court agree or disagree. Read Harry Golden's views on the case. Be prepared to explain your views and your reasons for agreement or disagreement with positions expressed.*

Getting In

by Dwight Pickard

When spring returns, can the siege of public golf courses be far behind? Mobs of golfers jockeying for tee-off times . . . foursomes packed together like spawning salmon . . . errant drives whistling over your head.

While at the pedigree-ed private country clubs the scene is lullabye peaceful. Mannered caddies treating you with respect . . . all the amenities observed . . .nobody swiping your new Titlist ball out of the rough and replacing it with one of their Acme seconds. After the round, the clubhouse, with plenty of creature comforts . . . business deals cemented with a round of drinks . . . chits to sign, not cash on the line, not to mention all the extras, a swimming pool, good food, the right people.

While whom you know is important, where you apply for membership also depends, of course, on who you are, what you want, and what you can pay.

At Gulph Mills it might help to know retired railroad man Stuart T. Saunders, or Bicentennial ringmaster Henderson Supplee, both of whom are members. It would also be helpful to be an Episcopalian or a Quaker, and to be unquestionably rich.

This club along with the Philadelphia C.C., Merion Cricket Club, the Radnor Hunt Club, Sunnybrook C.C., the Germantown Cricket Club, Huntington Valley C.C., and Philmont C.C., are described in E. Digby Baltzell's book, *Philadelphia Gentlemen,* as "the more exclusively upper class clubs." Green Valley, despite its cost, didn't make the list. Green Valley is predominantly Jewish.

At the opposite end of the socioeconomic scale is Sandy Run C.C. in Oreland, Pennsylvania. Known to its members as the "workingmen's club," it costs only $660 to join and about $250 a year for dues. The facilities are spartan—a banquet room, some showers, and a card room—but the people who belong there play from dawn to dusk, and that's all that counts.

Reprinted by permission of the *Philadelphia Inquirer,* February 21, 1971.

Then there are clubs with a few blue-collar workers but a preponderance of medium-income professionals. These include Melrose C.C. and Cedarbrook C.C., to which Italian-Americans gravitate, and Torresdale-Frankford, a neighborhood club which admits some Japanese, Korean, and Chinese members.

At Whitemarsh the membership is about 90 percent Irish-Catholic. At Northhills C.C. and Old York Road C.C. the memberships are a cross section of hard-working types who've made good and couldn't care less about not being in the Social Register.

Facilities at these and similar clubs range from plush to made-do. At Old York Road, for instance, there is a swimming pool and a dining room in addition to an 18-hole golf course. Bala C.C., off City Line Avenue, has a small clubhouse and no swimming pool; Torresdale-Frankford offers trapshooting ranges, an 18-hole golf course, a dining room, and steam baths.

But if you are black, you can plan on spending no money at all, because there are apparently no private clubs in the immediate Philadelphia area that accept black members. Blacks can caddy all they want, but they can't belong, not in Philadelphia. Where they can belong is at Freeway G.C. in Sickerville, New Jersey, where the membership is about 95 percent black.

Club May Exclude Anyone, Court Rules

by Don A. McDonough
of the *Inquirer* Staff

The Pennsylvania Superior Court, in a 4-3 decision, agreed Monday that a fraternal club may exclude anyone it chooses—even if the exclusion is on the basis of race.

The court upheld a ruling by Dauphin County Common Pleas Court, which overruled a Pennsylvania Human Relations Commission finding that Moose Lodge 107 in Harrisburg had violated the

Reprinted by permission of the *Philadelphia Inquirer,* December 14, 1971.

Ethnic associations provide members with the companionship of those with similar background and interests.

law when it refused service to a party that included State House of Representatives Majority Leader K. Leroy Irvis, a Pittsburgh Democrat.

The decision had no effect on a ruling by a three-judge panel in Middle district Federal Court, which held that the issuance of a liquor license to the lodge by the Pennsylvania Liquor Control Board violated the equal protection clause of the 14th Amendment because of the lodge's policy of discriminating against blacks.

Irvis, who is black, said the refusal of service in December 1968 was because of his race. He filed a complaint with the Human Relations commission.

The commission found the lodge was a "place of public accommodations" as defined in the 1955 Human Relations Act and that it was guilty of "unlawfully discriminating against Irvis." It issued a cease and desist order which the club appealed to the Dauphin County Court.

The county court held that, although the incident was "morally indefensible and that the conduct of the representatives and agents was deficient in good manners and common sense . . . the redress does not fall within the public accommodations section of the act."

Social, cultural, and patriotic purposes bring together members of ethnic organizations.

Only in America

by Harry Golden

Who is crowding the door?

That is the question a three-judge Federal District Court did not ask when it ruled that fraternal organizations, in this instance the Benevolent Protective Order of Elks, must cease discriminatory membership requirements or forfeit their tax-exemption privileges.

Does, however, Congresswoman Bella Abzug want to join the Ladies Auxiliary of the local American Legion Post?

Is William Buckley, editor of the "National Review," fighting for the chance to become a dues-paying member of the B'nai B'rith?

Do I want to attend meetings of the Charlotte, North Carolina branch of the Women's Christian Temperance Union or rule as parliamentarian at the convention of the Sons of the American Revolution?

Reprinted by permission of the *Philadelphia Jewish Times,* February 10, 1972.

I know that the membership of the Elks probably numbers in the millions. I have never, however, met a boy who wanted to grow up to become an Elk.

Thus I am not sure that blacks want wholesale admission to this fraternity. I do not know any Seventh-Day Adventist who wants to join.

To be sure, there are a variety of community interests the Elks serve and probably many blacks and Seventh-Day Adventists want to realize these interests too. Membership restrictions prohibit blacks from becoming Elks and Seventh-Day Adventists do not want to join. If the BPOE must remove discriminatory membership clauses, I seriously doubt that the Order will radically change.

Some years ago, the administration at Princeton insisted that the clubs, the fraternity system on campus, had to extend invitations to every incoming freshman. No one was to be excluded. Fifty percent of the students accepted the invitation to join. This was the usual percentage. The clubs are no longer exclusive but the membership is the same.

A New York judge has ruled that Mrs. Bernice Gera cannot be denied a job as a baseball umpire because of her sex. I do not think her presence behind the plate will appreciably change the national pastime. The lady jockey up in New York did not change the morning line.

The sit-in demonstrations of the 60s started in Charlotte. College boys picketed public accommodations for the right to be served. Within a day, they had won the point. The cafeteria managers and the drugstore fountain proprietors did not want stools and chairs occupied by dissenters. They did not want the public as bystanders but as customers.

But George Ivey, one of the most prosperous merchants in Charlotte (and in the South), balked. He did not want blacks in his exclusive Rainbow Room atop the Ivey Department Store.

"George," argued the civil righters, "how many black businessmen in Charlotte want to pay $8 for a cheese sandwich in the Rainbow Room? And how often? Who is crowding the Rainbow Room door?"

Finally George gave in and to this very day the Rainbow Room is so empty at high noon you can shoot deer in it.

May Quotas Help Get Minorities In?

Highly qualified members of minority groups and women often have not been hired in the past and are still refused admittance to many private organizations and institutions because of traditional discriminatory practices. Businesses, unions, and universities have created unofficial ethnic and sexist institutions which granted opportunity only to members of their own groups. When minorities were admitted it often was on the basis of a quota system, a discriminatory tool to limit numbers of certain groups to small percentages, so that most would be kept *out*. This persistent discrimination gave rise to a government policy known as *affirmative action,* a policy designed to get minorities and women *in*.

Executive Orders Numbers 4 and 11246 signed by President Lyndon Johnson in 1965 were issued to force institutions to give preferential treatment to women and minorities in school admission, hiring, and promotion practices. Minorities were defined as blacks, American Indians, Orientals, persons with Spanish surnames, and women, but not Greeks, Italians, Irish, Poles, not Catholics or Jews, nor others with social disadvantages such as members of low-income groups. The executive orders cover public schools, universities, civil services (police, fire, and other government agencies), construction and trade industries, unions, and private corporations and businesses employing more than twenty-five people. Those who do not comply were subject to court orders and/or withdrawal of government financial aid or contracts (many businesses receive from the government orders for all kinds of goods and services). Evidence of good faith in the hiring and promotion of minorities were the use of goals—percentages of Puerto Ricans, Mexican-Americans, women, and others—in the institution and timetables by which these groups entered. These percentages, many claim, amount to quotas. Defenders of affirmative action insist that the term quota is not used, but goals and timetables are the practical methods by which reluctant and long-discriminating institutions may be evaluated in regard to their compliance with nondiscrimination practices.

The questions raised by affirmative action are many. Two important ones are: In reviewing qualification tests and admission practices can we admit greater numbers of minorities and women without lowering reasonable standards? Can we reach out, go beyond the destruction of racist and sexist barriers, and encourage the integration of groups into the educational and occupational worlds without reverse discrimination against others? The reading selections that follow address themselves to these questions. *Determine the writers' answers. What do you think?*

"You Can't Quota-Out the Majority"

by Murray Friedman

Dr. Friedman is regional director of the American Jewish Committee and teaches courses on minority groups and urban sociology at LaSalle College.

Racial quotas as a means of bringing about desegregation has emerged as the sleeper issue of 1972. Before positions become hardened completely, it is important to understand why it is necessary to oppose quotas while supporting affirmative action programs that do not polarize the community further.

Persistent discrimination against blacks and other minorities and their small numbers in colleges and universities, government agencies and business organizations have given rise to a movement to hire or admit minorities on the basis of their number in the population or geographic area. Federal agencies have threatened

Reprinted by permission of the *Philadelphia Evening Bulletin,* December 3, 1972.

withdrawal of government contracts unless these institutions show a better racial balance through the use of racial goals and timetables which have, in effect, often amounted to quotas.

In Philadelphia, the issue has gained wide public attention in connection with the Philadelphia Plan to broaden involvement of blacks in the construction industry and the decision of Judge Fullam last May, now on appeal, temporarily prohibiting the police department from hiring or promoting except on the basis of one black for every two whites.

Schools and Universities

Less noticed has been the quiet institutionalization of the quota system in public schools, colleges and universities. One school at a Philadelphia university has had a 50 percent quota—it calls this a goal—for several years. At another institution here, the word went down at one point in one department that the next two appointees should be black. In practice, this was found to be unpracticable.

Quotas have become a source of racial confrontation. City College in New York several years ago was closed down and the president forced to resign following violence between low-income white ethnic and black students growing out of a proposed quota arrangement.

The Jewish community has felt particularly threatened by quotas. Adults remember when they were used as a means of keeping them out or limiting their admission to educational institutions. Less than 3 percent of the population and, because of discrimination and ethnic style, concentrated in certain fields of work, many feel vulnerable to any hiring or admission system that is not based on merit and qualifications.

In meeting with administration officials this year, Jewish agencies expressed their concern about quotas while indicating support for other affirmative action efforts. In August, President Nixon announced (as did Senator McGovern) opposition to quotas and ordered department heads "to ensure compliance with these views."

Black leaders such as Congressman Louis Stokes, chairman of the Congressional Black Caucus, saw this as yet another pullback from the national commitment to open housing, and linked it to abandonment of school desegregation efforts through slogans like "forced busing."

Group Against Group

The tragedy of the quota fight is that it is pitting group against group and, frequently, the poor against the near poor in a competition for scarce places that feeds a "white backlash." Affirmative action programs are needed that can bring about racial progress while at the same time minimizing community opposition.

A way out of the City College impasse was found by "enlarging the pie"—initiating an "open admissions" program providing free higher education for all those who desire it. Large numbers of low-income Italians, Poles and other ethnic groups have benefited as well as blacks and Puerto Ricans. The scarcity of doctors and lawyers, especially in the black community, cries out for new and imaginative ways of training. Some have called for hiring one apprentice for every four construction workers. Law could be read at the foot of practicing attorneys.

The University of Indiana Medical School has increased significantly its classes through special training programs.

We need to review qualification and tests to ensure they are relevant to job or admission needs. A considerably higher proportion of blacks passed the Pennsylvania bar examination last year when such a review was completed. The city of Philadelphia has announced plans to revise its police entrance examinations and training programs to eliminate any question of racial bias.

Special Efforts

Other affirmative action programs should include special efforts to identify and recruit qualified or qualifiable members of excluded groups and, where necessary, assist them to rise to a level where they can compete equally.

It is reasonable to expect that a more conservative Supreme Court will strike down quota arrangements. Like reparations and busing, quotas is a "no win" issue since it turns actual or potential allies into enemies of racial progress. As Richard Scammon, co-author of "The Real Majority," pointed out recently in commenting on the defeat of Senator McGovern, "you can't quota-out the majority."

No Group Served by Quota System

by Smith Hempstone

"Common sense and tradition would suggest that a university need not base its admission policy solely on academic standing. Character, personality, motivation, career potential, work experience, economic status, geographic distribution and racial origin may rightfully be used as criteria to select among applicants otherwise equal intellectually, or nearly so.

"But to reserve places for applicants *only* on the ground that they are members of one ethnic group or another clearly discriminates against those who do not happen to belong to that group. This flies in the face of any sense of fairness, contravenes [goes against] the Fourteenth Amendment and clearly must be unconstitutional."

And that, in essence, is what the Supreme Court ruled in *Bakke v. Board of Regents:* Allan Bakke must be admitted to the medical school of the University of California at Davis; the practice of reserving a specific number of places for any ethnic group is unconstitutional; but it is lawful for race to be one of the factors a university considers in a positive way when admitting a student.

That the court's 5-4 decision disappoints extremists on both sides of the dispute serves only to underline its basic fairness and logic. Some leaders of minorities would like to see large and rigid quotas to guarantee for their members that which they cannot obtain by merit. Some very conservative people would insist on that which

Adapted and printed from the (New Jersey) *Camden Courier Post,* July 6, 1978, with the permission of Smith Hempstone.

has never been—selection solely on the grounds of academic grades. Both are wrong.

Quotas not only are unfair, unAmerican and unworkable, they are laughable. If, as the Davis campus maintained, 16 percent of each medical school class must be blacks, chicanos or Asians, what percentage must be Irish, Italians or Wasps? How many must be red-headed or left-handed? What proportion should be able to play the flute?

To say that so many students must be admitted on the grounds of their color is just as racist as asserting that none may be admitted because of it. . . . By the same token, to pretend there is not in this country a disfiguring inheritance of past discrimination against some minorities—particularly blacks—is simply to deny the evidence that confronts us. Moreover, the government has a compelling interest in correcting the distortions and inequities that persist.

But one wrong cannot be righted by committing another. Ways have to be found—and are being found every day—to give the disadvantaged a fairer shake without discriminating against those who may have faced and surmounted equally difficult obstacles (the 38-year-old Bakke hardly was born with a silver spoon in his mouth: his father was a mailman; he worked his way through university on a Navy scholarship).

The people understand this, even if bureaucrats and racists— black or white—do not. Nobody wants to confine anyone to the back of the bus. But the majority of the people are equally determined there will be no reserved seats on the bus.

Blacks in Bakke Protest Defend Affirmative Action

by Steven V. Roberts
Special to *The New York Times*

Washington, Oct. 3—James Rudasill, son of a furniture repairman, was born in Shelby, N.C., a mill town where the schools were segregated. Today he is a second-year law student at George

Archibald Cox, attorney for the University of California in *Bakke* case, leaves Supreme Court. Courtesy Wide World Photos.

Washington University, admitted under a program that gives special preference to disadvantaged students, mostly blacks. Last year he was admitted; about 20 seats out of a class of 400 were reserved for students with lower test scores.

Mr. Rudasill was one of several hundred students who joined a march today protesting the lawsuit of Allan Bakke, the man who contends that he was unfairly rejected by the medical school of the University of California at Davis because preference was being given to racial minorities.

Ralph Chappell, another second-year law student, commented: "It doesn't affect me; I'm already in school, but my younger brother or the kids in my old neighborhood might also want to go into law."

If affirmative action programs that favor minorities exclude some whites like Mr. Bakke from professional schools, they give blacks like Mr. Rudasill their only chance.

The young man's parents, who never finished high school, moved north to Washington seeking better jobs and better education for their five children. James Rudasill, the star athlete and a good student, went to Brown University in Providence, R.I. His grades at

Brown were "mediocre," he concedes, partly because he worked as a janitor to finance his education.

"The education I got," said Mr. Chappell, the son of a community organizer, "was practically nonexistent, and I've been playing catch-up ever since. For instance, we never had a teacher who went deeply into the fundamentals of English with us. The students were all running around getting high, and the teachers were just worried about keeping us in class. So when it came to the test, it was just a guessing game for me."

In his younger days, Mr. Chappell ran with a street gang and had brushes with the law. On his way home from a college exam he was arrested falsely for armed robbery, and the experience pointed him toward the law. "I want to be in a position to protect my family and friends," he said.

Carolyn Perry grew up in Washington, D.C., the daughter of a government official who monitors affirmative action programs. But even as a middle-class black, Miss Perry feels she could not compete equally with whites.

"My parents did all they could; I went to the ballet and things like that, but there was a certain difference they couldn't make up for," said Miss Perry, who is 23 and a third-year student at George Washington University.

After getting her degree, she would like to work in government for a few years and then open a legal clinic in the black community.

"There are so few black professionals in this country, and there is a great need for them." Miss Perry asserted. "They say that affirmative action plans deprive whites of a place in law school, but are those whites going to go back and help the people who need help? There aren't enough people's lawyers, and this program is trying to bring in people who are interested in doing that."[1]

[1] Two recent Supreme Court decisions concerning affirmative action will shape the future of these programs. In the *Bakke* decision the Court ruled that the practice of reserving a *specific* number of places for any ethnic group in higher education is unconstitutional; however, race *is* a legitimate factor for preference in entrance into colleges. In the *Kaiser Aluminum and Chemical Corporation* v. *Weber* decision concerning the use of quotas and separate seniority lists for blacks and whites in the areas of job and job-training programs, the Court ruled that such affirmative action programs *are* constitutional.

Thought Twisters Relating to Educational and Job Opportunity

One writer commented: We have come to recognize that "competence" does not reside in high I.Q. score alone. There is also commitment, understanding, compassion, character, integrity, and the ability to relate. A white middle-class student with a 4.0 average will not necessarily make a better social worker, lawyer, doctor, teacher, than a black or brown with a 3.0. The long-range aim is to avoid the crystallization of our social structure into a sort of caste system—with blacks, Mexican-Americans, and others doing the unskilled menial work for an elite of white professionals and business managers.

Do you agree with this comment?

It is naive to think that laws and regulations will at once eliminate prejudice and discrimination in employment and education. And more naive and hypocritical to label affirmative action a form of "reverse racism." Religious and ethnic bias is too deeply engrained in the American system to be outlawed by a stroke of a pen. Employers, administrators, educators, and government officials are too resourceful to let minorities get more than a token foothold in the system. Goals and timetables are practical ways of getting minorities in.

Could employers show their faith without goals and timetables? Are these quotas?

It is ridiculous to argue that because this ethnic group has x percent of the population they should have x percent of the jobs or seats in college. This is self-defeating nonsense, for no person of ability wants to be limited in his or her horizons by an arbitrary quota or wants to endure unqualified people in positions that they fill only because of a numerical racial quota.

What is a fair share of jobs or admissions? What should be used to measure good faith in admissions?

Moreover, while assuredly most people of color in this country are culturally disadvantaged, not all are, nor are all whites by any stretch of the imagination properly to be considered "advantaged." Rarely, if ever, for instance, have whites from Appalachia been singled out as a group for preferential educational treatment.

> Should all those who bear scars of economic and cultural discrimination receive preferential treatment as a form of restitution? Do you think discrimination against minorities of color has been specially severe?

Women have entered the occupational race in this country with their feet tied by discrimination. Men have been able to rush forward in the race with both feet free. Now those who cry against reverse discrimination only want to cut the bonds that tie women's feet. We say something has to be done to make up for all the time we were hobbling.

> Is it proper to correct imbalances without using a form of reverse discrimination? Should a present discriminatory practice be used to correct past discrimination?

I have only one worthwhile thing to give: my trade. I hope to follow a centuries-old tradition and sponsor my sons for apprenticeship. For this simple father's wish it is said that I discriminate against Negroes. Don't all of us discriminate? Which of us when it comes to a choice will not choose a son over all others? I believe that an apprenticeship in my union is no more a public trust, to be shared by all, than a millionaire's money is a public trust.

> A number of craft unions made up of workers with specialized skills have become, for historical reasons, dominated by members of one ethnic group. They see the union and with it the job as a means of providing their relatives and friends with a living. How would you answer the writer above who justifies such a policy?

Al Smith campaigned for the presidency in 1928 but was unable to overcome religious prejudice. Why do you think John F. Kennedy was successful in 1960 in spite of his religion? Courtesy of The Bettmann Archive, Inc.

SECTION FOUR

Ethnicity as Expressed in Political Behavior

Compared to the native-born American, the immigrant had many disadvantages: less income, less desirable job, less status, and less knowledge of the country and its ways. But once he became a citizen, the newcomer became the equal of the native-born in one important way: he had a vote. As the population of new Americans increased, political parties and their candidates began to seek immigrant support. How would the immigrants vote: as individuals or as members of ethnic groups? Joined together in residence, in organizations, and frequently in occupations, and also bound by cultural ties, it seemed natural for the newcomers to vote as their fellows voted. American politics has been based on the expression of group interests—economic, geographic, and ethnic—each group often competing with one another to get benefits for itself. New Americans, urged by their leaders and ethnic press, came to realize that by sticking together, the combined impact of their votes would make itself felt.

Some writers make it seem as if it were unpatriotic to vote for one's self-interests. But suppose a candidate were unfriendly to bankers—would it be natural or even reasonable for bankers to vote for him? Newcomers looked for those candidates and parties that they believed favored them. Doing this, they performed no differently than did the farmers, industrialists, businessmen, and workingmen before them—and since. Theme Nine explores politics as expressions of group interests. Topic 24 has you examine political parties as coalitions of interest groups.

What were the needs of the immigrants? The newcomers required jobs, and in many instances these jobs came from political bosses. Topic 25 offers a view of big-city bosses and their

169

"machines" that differ from that pictured by standard American history textbooks. Unlike Thomas Nast, the political cartoonist who drew one boss as a huge vulture preying upon the city treasury, the immigrant view of city politics was friendlier. The data in this topic focuses on the relationship between the influx of immigrants in the late nineteenth and early twentieth centuries and the rise of big-city bosses.

Their American experience developed certain broad political attitudes on the part of ethnic groups descended from the "new immigration" whose majorities fell in the working class located in cities. This experience, contrasted with that of earlier immigrants, provides the focus of the next topic.

Topic 27 asks you to interpret data just as a political scientist does. It demonstrates devices used to determine the voting patterns of ethnic groups and suggests that ethnic bloc (group) voting may not be dead. Topics 26 and 27 illustrate conceptual Theme Ten, that ethnicity is a major factor at the polls.

Power lies at the heart of politics—power to shape and control the behavior of others. Often power becomes the means of achieving other goals such as wealth, prestige, or recognition. Topic 28 examines some reasons why an ethnic group wants its members in political office.

How does a minority group member get into political office? Topic 29 shows how minority group membership, often a barrier in the quest for political office, can serve, under certain conditions, as an aid to public office. Topics 28 and 29 illustrate the theme that ethnicity operates in public office.

When the immigrants landed in America they brought with them, locked in their memories, cultural and political "baggage" as well as physical baggage. Topics 30, 31, and 32 cluster about the theme that important public issues grow out of ethnic political behavior (Theme Twelve). Topic 30 provides samples of foreign-affairs issues. Ethnic groups do not forget brethren overseas. Topic 31 introduces you to a major national issue which grows out of the value system of a major religious group. The final topic helps to sum up the interrelationship between political behavior and ethnic background. It asks you to apply what you have learned to contemporary political situations and issues, with a particular focus on blacks and political action.

Politics Is an Expression of Group Interests

Presidential candidate William McKinley (front row, third from left) poses with an ethnic political group during his campaign. Courtesy of Ohio Historical Society.

How Did Political Parties Form?

It is the hypothesis of this study that group interests have shaped American politics. Nowhere is this more evident than in the formation of political parties and in political activities. Special-interest groups may be formed about occupations, such as farmers, teachers, truck drivers, and doctors. Class groupings such as upper, lower, middle, and working are formed about income and wealth. People may be grouped according to how they earn their living—as industrialists, bankers, storekeepers, owners of stock, managers, factory workers. Even people living in sections of the country may be grouped—as New Englanders, Southerners, and Mid-Westerners. All of these groups have common interests that lead them to preferences in party and voting. In the topics that follow we will see how ethnicity—the factors of race, religion, national origin, and immigration—influence politics.

To back up an hypothesis one must have evidence. What is the evidence that group interests have combined to form political parties? Take a look in American history textbooks and read about the formation of political parties. *Find out (1) the reasons why the party was formed and (2) which groups gathered to support them.* Consider the founding of the Federalist party, the Republican-Democratic party (Jeffersonian Democrats), the Republican party, and the Populist party.

What Was the Relationship of
Immigrants to Urban Politics?

In his book *The Bosses* Ralph G. Martin, a political journalist, explains why political leaders called "bosses" became popular in America's great cities in the latter part of the nineteenth century. To understand this reading you should know that the "boss" got his name from his control over the party organization called the "machine." This term came from the party's ability to win the loyalty of enough voters so that it could run over its opponents in election after election.

A party organization consisted of (and still does today) ward leaders, party officers from the various sections of the city. These ward leaders were called bosses too, for they dominated life in the neighborhoods they represented. Often the party boss of the city was a ward leader himself. Ward leaders selected and commanded party workers called committeemen, who lived among and influenced voters in a ward, an area of a few city blocks. The party boss and a few top ward leaders drew up the slates—candidates on the ballot for the many public offices to be elected by the voters—mayor, district attorney, judges, city councilmen, state senators and state representatives, and many others. Without the party's backing, without the aid of a party's faithful followers and workers who urge voters to the polls, a candidate would have little chance of getting elected. Those party-backed candidates once in office have obligations to the bosses.

What follows is a transcription of an interview with an immigrant who had close connection with a "boss." If possible it might be more interesting to hear on tape with someone impersonating the interviewee. Find out what relationship Italian immigrants had with this boss. Then read about Boston's Boss James Curley. Note (1) how and why he was able to achieve power and (2) how his rise to power was connected with immigrants. (3) Does anything remain today of the kind of politics that existed in Curley's time? If so, what is it and what is your evidence?

TRANSCRIPTION OF A TAPED INTERVIEW WITH VITO BALDI, SUMMER, 1970*

Narrator:

Vito Baldi, an elderly man in his late 70s, semi-retired from his funeral parlor business, recalls how he and his father aided the Italian immigrant in the 1920s.

Vito Baldi:

There were a number of businesses in which my father was engaged—the real-estate business, the coal business, the insurance business. My father operated one of the first Italian banks in the city of Philadelphia which aided immigrants entering here. By his connections with the Vare brothers, influential city politicians, he was able to obtain employment for the immigrants in the various city departments, usually in the street cleaning, water, and city building departments. The work was menial, but what could the immigrant do? I remember going to William Vare's office, where Mr. Vare would give an immigrant his card with a little note on it. This was the same as an assignment to a job. The Vares never refused one who applied and the Italians were grateful.

My father was interested in having schools in the Italian section of this city. There was a little school on Carpenter Street between 9th and 10th. Poorly constructed, it lacked fire proofing, and was overcrowded with students. My father called on George Vare, asking him to do something. He said, "Well, Charley, if you are interested in that we will put you on the school board; then you can make your own arrangements." Well, among the schools built were a high school at 11th and Catherine, a school at 8th and Fitzwater,

*Mr. Baldi died a few years after this interview.

Southern High, and a number of others. My father also had the Italian language taught in the public schools in 1930.

Boss James M. Curley

Curley became chairman of the Democratic War Committee by a seven-vote margin in 1900. At age 26 he was the youngest ward boss in the city. His ward, Ward 17, became known as the Tammany ward because Curley had visited New York, studied the Tammany organization (Democratic party of New York City) in great detail, and even named his ward political club the Roxbury Tammany Club. The ward held meetings in a worn-out tenement building which had a sign with a surefire slogan: GET JOBS FOR THE BOYS.

Curley learned a great deal from Boston boss Lomasney of the West End. He copied Lomasney's techniques with immigrants. For the brand new citizen at the turn of the century the confusion of the ballot was almost incredible. Immigrants from southern and central Europe had almost no knowledge of the methods of free government, and the immigrants from Ireland viewed all government as suspect, for the Irish were ruled by the English. These newcomers were confronted with a ballot of 334 candidates for several dozen offices. Curley held election classes for immigrant voters and handed them each a comb with broken teeth, broken in such a way that, when placed on the ballot, it covered all the opposition candidates and exposed Curley's favorites. He also perfected another trick: an illiterate voter would claim he left his glasses at home and couldn't see without them and a Curley man would kindly escort him to the election booth and read the names of the candidates to him.

For Ward 17 the early 1900s proved a time of turmoil. Into it (and into the East's large cities) poured the immigrants—poor, strangers in a strange land. If arrested for peddling without a

Adapted from Ralph G. Martin, *The Bosses* (New York: Putnam, 1964), pp. 214–217, 219, 226–227.

The Honorable James Curley of Boston. Courtesy The Bettmann Archive, Inc.

license, or found drunk and disorderly, or mistaken for a thief, to whom could the immigrant turn? His English was poor, his purse small, his terror real. Who could help him and why should anyone bother?

Then the immigrant found the Boss, or, more likely, the Boss found him. For the immigrant did have a valuable asset—his vote. If the Boss could deliver the votes of the poor to elect public officials friendly to business interests, the latter could in turn reward the Boss with graft, a portion of which could be used to meet the welfare needs of the poor voters.

For Curley and bosses like him, there were no hours and no privacy. Curley kept his door open, his ear and his advice and specific help available. For these people no politician could pay off in promises. The payoff had to be specific and visible. Curley got pushcart licenses for peddlers, pursuaded landlords to delay evictions, got those in trouble out of jail, found funds for widows' funerals and burial expenses, arranged for tubercular patients to get to hospitals, filed citizenship papers, gave Thanksgiving baskets and Christmas food baskets and tons of coal to warm the immigrants' winter. He yelled the loudest, and for his ward got sanitary plumbing for the school buildings and a gym for the kids to keep them off the roofs. For the forgotten man here was somebody that really cared.

The beauty of the Boss was that there was no red tape, no forms to fill out, no months of waiting for interviews with social workers and repeated questioning by prying, unsympathetic investigators. When Curley said something, it happened; when he promised something, you got it fast.

Curley went to extreme lengths to get jobs for voters in his ward. In 1903, while running for city council, the lawmaking branch of government, he aided a ward worker who wanted to be a letter carrier but did not feel capable of passing the civil service test. Posing as the applicant, Curley took the test, passed it with high marks, but was spotted, reported, and sentenced to sixty days in the Charles Street Jail. He won the council seat campaigning from jail.

When James M. Curley became mayor of the city of Boston he went into action, and the city had its broadest face-lifting of the century. Playgrounds replaced slums, tunnels and transit systems traversed the city, streets widened, paved sidewalks appeared, and hospitals and schools seemed to pop up everywhere. Everybody in Boston seemed to be working again even if they had such specialized jobs as "Tea Warmers," or "Rubber-boot Repairers," or "Wipers" or "Tree Climbers." The immigrants, untrained and unskilled, rushed to fill the jobs created by the big building programs and city improvements. The businessmen who received profitable contracts, licenses, tax favors, and friendly law enforcement from the Curley administration were ready to honor notes such as this one from Curley:

> The bearer, Mr. O'Brien of Roxbury, who is the father of a large family, is very much in need of some sort of work to provide for them. Will you use your good offices with some one of the contractors doing work for the city who might be able to put him to work as a watchman?

His opponents claimed that Curley was getting kickbacks (sums of money for favors granted) from contractors building for the city, and the more projects the mayor started the more kickbacks he got. Such accusations did not bother the immigrants at all; they remembered Curley at the polls.

Ethnicity Is a Major Factor at the Polls

Political posters make a special appeal to voters in ethnic neighborhoods at election time.

TOPIC 26

How Does Ethnicity Influence
Party Preference?

In the last topic you learned how political parties try to meet
the needs of group interests. You studied the special needs of the
new immigrants to the city. In this topic we will examine the needs
of the sons and daughters of these immigrants and how past experiences influence political preference. The first reading selection that
follows, written by Samuel Lubell, describes the background of foreign stock, those born in a foreign country or having at least one
parent born in a foreign country. The conclusions Lubell reaches are
a result of his study of election returns and a close examination of
ethnic groups from southern and eastern Europe, largely Catholic
and Jewish. He defines the Roosevelt Coalition, a bundle of interest
groups which held together for thirty years.

The second reading concerns an ethnic group that does not
consider itself an ethnic group at all! However, its members are very
well represented in the Republican party, and most hold to a basic
value system which shapes their preference.

As you examine these two selections, look for information that
will help you answer these questions: *What led these ethnic groups
toward political parties? What shapes an ethnic group's view of
government?*

The third learning experience has you examine a table. The
table is based on a Connecticut study of blue-collar and white-collar
workers. The blue-collar group is made up of working-class people
having occupations from highly skilled craftsmen, semiskilled oper-
atives, construction and transportation workers to unskilled laborers. White-collar workers include clerks and sales people as well as
business executives and professional people such as doctors and

lawyers. Generally, the income of white-collar workers is higher, and a large number of these workers make up the high middle and upper classes. *What statements can you make about occupational class, ethnicity, and political party preference by examining this table? In what way is the table related to the readings?*

The Roosevelt Coalition

The "new immigration" after 1885, which crowded the teeming cities, came mainly from Italy, Poland, Russia, Greece, and the disintegrating Austro-Hungarian Empire. The larger part of these new immigrants were Catholic, but they also included 1.5 million Jews.

Because they came to this country late, these immigrants and their children were concentrated in the lower economic rungs. Moreover, they resented what seemed to be efforts to force conformity to an Anglo-Saxon, Protestant culture. This was evidenced by the passage of Sunday Blue Laws, which closed businesses related to recreation; prohibition, which stopped the sale of liquor; and the growth of the Klu Klux Klan with its campaigns against immigrants, Jews and Catholics as well as blacks.

Throughout the industrialized eastern part of the United States the makeup of society was such that Protestantism coincided largely with the Republican party, with factory owners and bankers, with snobbish members of exclusive clubs—in short—with the upper classes. Catholicism, in turn, coincided largely with discrimination and unskilled labor, with immigrant minorities who were looked down upon as inferior beings—in short—the lower classes.

The conditions under which these immigrants worked and lived hardly requires description here. Upon their arrival circumstances thrust them into those parts of the economy with the sorest tensions—the unsanitary factories, the dangerous mines—into the sweatiest jobs where wages just about enabled them to survive and

Adapted from Samuel Lubell, *The Future of American Politics* (New York: Harper & Brothers, 1952), pp. 32–33, 36, 39, 46.

President-elect Franklin D. Roosevelt leans over to chat with President Herbert Hoover on inauguration day, 1933. How did the new president differ in his attack on the Depression from his predecessor? Courtesy Franklin D. Roosevelt Library.

where labor unions had no power. The foreign born made up 60 percent of the workers in the packinghouse plants described so well by Upton Sinclair's novel *The Jungle;* 57 percent of those in iron and steel, 61 percent of our miners, and nearly 70 percent of those toiling in textiles or clothing.

No matter what else had happened, the growing up of these children of the 13 million immigrants who poured into the country between 1900 and 1914 was bound to have a great influence on American society. As it was, the Great Depression—striking in 1929 when most of them had barely entered the adult world— sharpened all their memories of childhood hardships. When Franklin Roosevelt first took office in 1933, no segment of the population was more ready for a "new deal" than the kept-down, silent city masses. They became the chief carriers of the Roosevelt program of change.

Never having known anything but city life, this new generation developed a different attitude toward the role of government from that of Americans born on farms and in small towns. To Herbert Hoover, president from 1929 to 1933, rugged individualism, self-reliance, and government "hands-off" policy brought memories of a thrifty, toiling farmer who made most of his own things, grew most of his own food, and had jars and barrels of food laid away for the winter.

In the city, life differed. The worker depended completely on a money wage. Without a job there were no vegetables for his family, no bread, no rent, and no fuel. He was completely dependent on the boss and the job. A political program that called for "leaving things alone" to work themselves out, as espoused by Herbert Hoover, seemed either unreal or downright cruel in the cities where every condition groaned for reform. The wage earner had to look to the government to make sure that the milk bought for his baby was not watered or tubercular; he had to look to government to regulate the construction of tenements so that all the sunlight was not blocked out. If only God could make a tree, only the government could make a park. The New Deal, as the administration of Franklin Roosevelt was called, promised a great deal of government action and reform.

By 1935 the working class had a feeling of loyalty to each other and to the New Deal. The Great Depression (1929–1939), in making all workers aware of their economic interests, suppressed their racial and religious hatreds. Put crudely, the hatred of bankers and the rich industrialists among the native-born workers of native-born parents had become greater than their hatred of the Pope or even of blacks. Now blacks, native-American workers, and foreign-stock workers joined together to become the central pivot of all those diverse interests called the Roosevelt Coalition which supported the Democratic party.

The Republicans and the Protestants

Anglo-Saxon Protestants are a group which does not think of itself as an ethnic group at all. When questioned as to their identity, members answer simply, "American," as well they might, for their ancestors founded and settled the nation, and dominated its political, social, and economic life until the 1920s. Anglo-Saxon Protes-

Written by Philip Rosen, instructor in history, Northeast High School, Philadelphia, PA.

tants, sometimes called "old-American stock," are a product of widespread intermarriage. The Scotch, Germans, Dutch, and Scandinavians, all immigrants from northern Europe, were amalgamated into the original British society in America. These people became the bedrock strength of the Republican party.

Voting behavior is a product of subconscious as well as conscious forces. The thrust of a great deal of Protestant religious thinking has been freedom for the individual for a direct encounter with God without the restraint of group controls and loyalties. Protestants generally elevate the individual and denounce the tribalism of the group. By stressing individualism the Protestant position in politics has been, historically, to discourage the government from interfering with the individual. This is a policy of laissez-faire: let the people alone to work out things for themselves—keep government out of business—no government projects or programs, even for the disadvantaged. Protestant location in rural America or among the well-to-do classes in the cities reinforced their idea that poor conditions among city industrial workers were a result of the latter's lack of initiative and the presence of other poor character traits which could be overcome by individual effort. The larger number conceive of good government as honest, efficient, run by professionals who do not stray too far from established principles—a government which does not get into debt or spend too much. The slogan of the campaign of 1884—"Rum, Romanism, and Rebellion"—did not win the Republicans the presidential election, but the spirit it conveyed, that of identifying the Democratic party with a position proliquor, pro-Catholic, and prosocial change, has kept a loyal contingent of Protestant voters casting straight Republican ballots.

It would be unfair to present the Grand Old Party as homogeneous as white milk. Great shifts are taking place in party allegiance. Disgusted with taxation, integration, and faulty social-welfare programs, white ethnics among the city descendants of later immigrant groups are moving toward Republican viewpoints. Protestants in suburbia just outside the city, secure in their livelihood and status, may vote for liberal Democrats. Responding to the needs of local voters, the Republican party in different areas of the country may abandon conservative positions to support more government intervention on behalf of the aged, the education of the young, and lower- and middle-income groups. Although some ethnic factors that influence party choice can be identified, the bulk of the American people are either independent or only weakly loyal to political parties.

ETHNICITY, OCCUPATIONAL CLASS, AND POLITICAL PARTY
PREFERENCE
(in percent)

Religio-ethnic group	White-collar	Blue-collar	Political party preference		
			Dem.	Rep.	Ind.
blacks (all religions)	13	87	86	7	7
Protestants (white)	48	52	38	45	17
Jews	75	25	81	8	11
Catholics (white)	36	64	70	16	14
Specific Catholic groups					
Irish	49	51	75	26	21
Italian	36	64	73	18	9
Polish	22	78	64	15	21
Spanish-speaking (mainly Puerto Rican)	5	95	87	10	3

Source: Harold J. Abramson, *Ethnic Pluralism in the Connecticut Central City,* (Storrs, Conn.: University of Connecticut, 1971).

How Can We Detect and Analyze the Voting Patterns of Ethnic Groups?

In the last learning experience you discovered how cultural values, past experiences, and work needs and habits of a class of people influenced ethnic groups in selecting a political party. In this experience the noted political analyst Samuel Lubell tells how he located ethnic groups in the Roosevelt Coalition and isolated the factors that motivated their voting preferences in selected elections. You will be asked to analyze the results and compare your interpretations with his.

Using some of Lubell's techniques, a study guide has been included which demonstrates how to examine relationships between ethnic-group membership and voting behavior. While the examples are taken from Philadelphia, the methods may be applied anywhere.

Before reading the Lubell selection you should know that a ward is a political division of a city enclosing many blocks. Election statistics are taken by wards as well as by precincts, a polling area of a few city blocks containing about 600 voters. If a ward or precinct happens to enclose a neighborhood with a heavy concentration of one ethnic group, you can already see the possibilities of election analysis. *Follow the directions as you read the selection and work on the study guide.*

Samuel Lubell Tells How He Did It

I set out to find out what were the major voting elements which Franklin Roosevelt brought together into victorious coalition. My first step was to analyze the election returns for each of more than 3,000 counties in the United States and for our major cities, ward by ward, in some areas getting down to precincts (election divisions). Few of these statistics appear in this text: I have used the election returns as tracer material akin to radioactive isotopes, through which the major voting streams and trends in the country could be isolated and followed in all their fluctuations from election to election.

Having sorted out the streams of voters who tend to shift together, I then did two other things. I poured through all the available library material, from census data to local histories, piecing together the distinctive economic, religious, cultural and political characteristics of these major voting elements. Finally, I spent many months traveling throughout the country, visiting strategic areas and talking to voters in every walk of life.

Here is a sample of some of the voting patterns I examined. It is, perhaps, the most vivid single illustration of the rhythm of ethnic emotions which vibrates through the Democratic majority. In Boston since 1928 all of the Democratic presidential candidates have received a bit more or less than two-thirds of the vote. Such statistical consistency gives the appearance of slight political change. Actually, the different Democratic elements have fluctuated furiously. The table which follows lists the ten wards with the highest Democratic percentage for each presidential election since 1928. When Al Smith (Irish Catholic) ran, the five top wards were predominately Irish (2,6,7,8, and 10); then came the largely Italian wards (1 and 3). The two most heavily Jewish wards (12 and 14) do not show up among the first Democratic ten in either 1928 or 1932. In 1936 the Irish wards drop, as Lemke, the isolationist candidate who promises not to go to war to support Britain, cuts into Roosevelt's vote, while the Italo-American and Jewish wards move to the top . . . .

*   *   *   *   *

Adapted from Samuel Lubell, *The Future of American Politics* (New York: Harper & Brothers, 1952), pp. 6, 211–214.

At this point we cut off Lubell's narrative and include a chart of Boston's wards. Examine the rankings of wards while you keep in mind their ethnic composition as Lubell has told you above. You should know that the American Irish are still angry at Britain over its past treatment of Ireland, and the division of that isle into a Protestant dominated Ulster and a Catholic free state in the south. *Analyze what happened in the ranking of the wards in 1940 and 1944.* Then compare your interpretation with Lubell's, which is printed just below. Keep in mind these events: In 1940 Roosevelt moves strongly to support Britain and her allies against Nazi Germany in World War II. Italy joins the side of Germany in the war. By 1944 Roosevelt becomes the leader of the world's forces against German, Japanese, and Italian fascism as news begins to reveal the extent of Nazi persecution of European Jews.

ORDER OF BOSTON WARDS MOST HEAVILY DEMOCRATIC

Rank	1928	1932	1936	1940	1944
1	2	2	14	14	14
2	6	6	3	2	12
3	7	7	1	6	2
4	10	1	2	12	6
5	8	8	6	7	9
6	1	10	7	8	7
7	3	3	8	9	8
8	15	15	12	1	11
9	11	11	15	15	10
10	13	13	11	11	15

Samuel Lubell's Interpretation

To sum up, the dissatisfaction of one element strengthens the attachments of other elements of the Democratic coalition. Although one cannot measure them statistically, the antagonism which runs through the alliance of various groups called the Roosevelt

Coalition is evident. The Irish and Germans respond favorably to isolationism, but this has been more than offset by the strong loyalty to Franklin Roosevelt's foreign policy by southerners, Jews, Polish-Americans, and other ethnic groups outraged by Hitler. To a remarkable extent the conflicting elements have tended to neutralize each other, so dissatisfaction by one ethnic group toward a policy is neutralized by the flocking to the Democratic banner of another ethnic group for that same policy.

PHILADELPHIA'S WARDS IN 1972

Directions: What does this map tell you about the different wards in the city of Philadelphia? Locate the 9th, 39th, and 54th wards. What are the street and other boundaries which encompass these wards? Use the information in the Study Guide section which follows to see if there is any ethnic pattern to voting in these wards.

STUDY GUIDE

_____
name   section

Directions: Keeping in mind that ward 9 is largely white Protestant, ward 39 largely Italian, and ward 54 largely Jewish, what can you say about the party preferences of these three ethnic groups in 1968? Use the information in the following chart to answer the questions below:

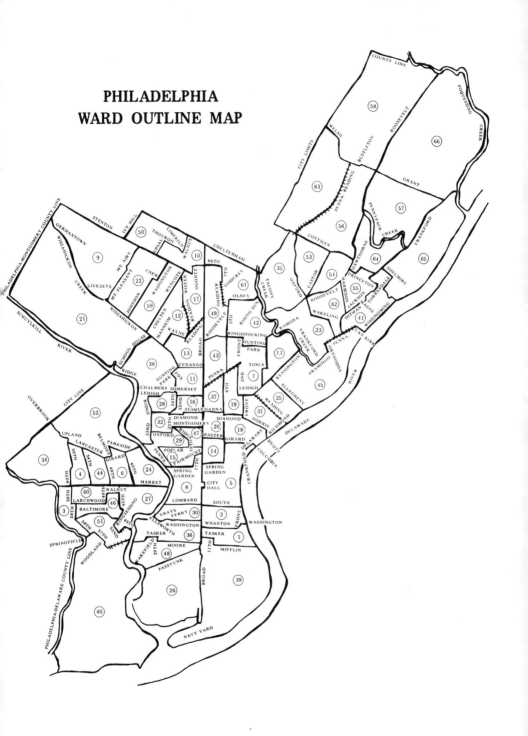

PHILADELPHIA
WARD OUTLINE MAP

CHART 1: REGISTERED VOTERS BY PARTY*

Ward number	Democrats	Republicans	Miscellaneous and nonpartisan	Grand total of registered voters
9	3,922	6,268	522	10,760
39	14,921	14,338	744	29,723
54	10,380	5,569	300	16,249

*A registered voter is one who has met the requirements for voting where he or she resides. One's name is on record as being eligible to vote. All data below refer to registered voters. "Miscellaneous" refers to minor parties, and "nonpartisan" means the voter does not wish to declare for any party.

1. According to this information most white Protestants tended in 1968 to register in which party? _____

2. In which party did most Jews register? _____

3. How did the Italians in ward 39 register? _____

4. What general statement can you make that accurately describes the relationship of ethnic groups to political parties in Philadelphia in 1968?
_____
_____
_____

CHART 2: VOTE FOR GOVERNOR OF PENNSYLVANIA, NOVEMBER 1970

Ward number	Republican Raymond Broderick (Catholic)	Democrat Milton Shapp (Jewish)
9	3,827	3,969
39	9,450	11,120
54	2,866	10,364
City total	232,567	410,606

5. What differences do you note between registration and voting in ward 54 in 1968 to 1970? _____

_____

_____

6. To what extent did the registration reflect the actual voting trend in the other two wards? _____

_____

_____

CHART 3: VOTE FOR MAYOR OF PHILADELPHIA IN GENERAL
ELECTION, NOVEMBER 1971

Ward number	Democrat Frank Rizzo (Italian)	Republican Thatcher Longstreth (white Protestant)
9	2,601	6,497
39	19,797	3,930
54	8,376	5,943
City total	391,692	343,168

7. What differences do you note between registration and voting in ward 39 in the mayorality election of 1971? (Note: The source for election statistics, the Registration Commission of the City of Philadelphia, reported no significant change in registration statistics in 1971.)

_____

_____

8. Describe voting patterns in the other two wards. _____

_____

_____

9. To what extent is there a connection in wards 39 and 54 between ethnicity and voting behavior? _____

_____

_____

Ethnicity Is a Factor in Political Office

Political campaigning is visible and active in ethnic neighborhoods at election time. Why do you think ethnics want their own to represent them?

Why Does an Ethnic Group Want
Its Own Members in Political Office?

We have studied how ethnic groups respond to parties, candidates, and office holders. The various groups react to what are felt needs and situations. The last topic indicated that certain ethnic groups will vote for their own members running for political office. *Why?* Although it is often claimed "the best man for the job," what happens when there are many "best men"? Those in women's liberation will state, "What about the best woman?" To secure representation for certain groups ethnic "seats" were created in many areas of American political life. For years the president appointed a Jew as a justice of the Supreme Court. Until recently whenever that member left the Court another Jewish person was appointed. Thurgood Marshall, chosen by President Johnson, was the first black on the Supreme Court. When he vacates that seat it will be interesting to see if another black is appointed.

Political parties are well aware of the factors of ethnicity in choosing candidates. Yet American voters are showing more and more sophistication in considering factors of merit and issues over that of ethnicity, although the practice of a "balanced ticket" still continues. In order to appeal to diverse people within a political constituency, members of diverse ethnic groups are chosen. Party leaders know that many Americans hold a number of prejudices, so that for certain offices, such as the presidency, no woman, nor black, nor eastern or southern European descendant has yet been chosen. In more local elections where such groups hold important blocs of votes, party leaders add such candidates to the ticket.

In the materials that follow, ethnic group members plea for a political "seat." What are the reasons, both stated and unstated, that such groups seek representation in political office? *Do you think that these are good reasons? Why or why not?*

Other Minorities Want a Share

To the Editor:

The recent announcement of persons named to the Bicentennial Commission is a direct slap in the face to many minority groups who helped build this nation. Only the blacks received their just due on the commission.

In a body of forty-three, ten blacks is a just and proper proportion—the blacks representing a quarter [sic] of our population.* But by the same token, Poles, representing six percent of the population, should have had at least two representatives appointed. None was.

Other ethnic groups that constitute high enough percentages of population should likewise have been given representation, while other smaller ethnic groups ought to have been amalgamated and permitted to choose proportionate representation of their own.

If the planners think their prestige is enough to make the Bicentennial celebration a success, they are dead wrong. Their arrogance is bound to polarize the ethnic groups against participation in and cooperation with the celebration plans. And then where will they be?

Joseph S. Wnukowski, President
Polish Heritage Society of
Philadelphia

Reprinted by permission of the *Philadelphia Inquirer,* March 13, 1971.

*Philadelphia's black population is approaching 40 percent. It was 35 percent by the 1970 census.

GOP Offering Broad Appeal, Balanced Statewide Ticket

Hempstead, L.I., June 11

The candidates on the ticket completed by party leaders and awaiting the formality of approval by the full Republican State Committee represent religious, racial, and national origin considerations. Completing the ticket are Harold A. Stevens, a black Catholic; Stephen May, a Protestant; and Louis Lefkowitz, a Jew. Much of the discussion on the balanced ticket among Republicans centered on the need to have an Italian American. Ralph G. Caso, the Republican Nassau County executive running for lieutenant governor, would fit the bill State Chairman Richard M. Rosenbaum stated in an interview. But Rosenbaum said the deciding factor was Mr. Caso's qualifications, experience, and proved vote-getting ability.

"I think there was a feeling I would help attract Italian-Americans to our ticket, and I would like to attract them," Mr. Caso said. State Senator John D. Calandra believed the Italian-American community would be happy to have one of their own "just a heartbeat away from being governor."

The above story is based on actual news article.

Corrigan to Safeguard Poles' Rights in Schools

by Ann Skinner

Daniel O. Corrigan, a lawyer as well as president of the Cleveland Board of Education, yesterday argued his own merits, by marriage, as a spokesman for ethnic interests on the school curriculum review committee.

The Ohio division of the Polish American Congress this week

Reprinted by permission of the *Cleveland Plain Dealer,* February 14, 1969.

registered its strong displeasure that no one from the heavily Polish southeast area was appointed to the committee.

"The Congress is contemplating rejecting the findings of this committee before its first meeting; to also encourage a boycott of the results; the possibility of encouraging a student boycott," said a statement from the group.

It continued: "The Congress expressed appreciation for a new comprehensive high school (South High) serving Southeast Cleveland by supporting school issues 9, 10 and 11 at the last election. The Congress is, nevertheless, also apprehensive about future curriculum offerings to students.

"Parents living in Southeast Cleveland also have inalienable rights to be represented on the curriculum review committees. For many years the Congress has been concerned about teaching Slav history and culture to the youth of Southeast Cleveland."

When asked if he would appoint a Polish spokesman to the committee, Corrigan said:

"The board president's wife is half Hungarian and half Slovak, so his children are half Irish, one-quarter Hungarian and one-quarter Slovak. His brother's wife is Polish.

"His wife's brother's wife is Polish. His wife's uncle's brother's wife is Polish, and the board president feels qualified to represent the inalienable rights of the Poles."

In a more serious vein Corrigan said: "We can't be using nationality as a yardstick. The appointments to the committee were not made on the basis of race, color or creed but on the basis of who, in the judgment of the president of the board, could best serve the curriculum committee at this time."

TRANSCRIPT OF TAPE-RECORDED INTERVIEW
WITH MRS. APONTE, SUMMER 1971

Narrator:

Mrs. Carmen Aponte is employed as a social service coordinator at the Council of Spanish-Speaking Organizations, 2023 N. Front Street, Philadelphia, Pennsylvania. A former school-

Mrs. Carmen Aponte

community coordinator at the Moffet Elementary School, Philadelphia, she is no stranger to school problems. Recently she testified at a Philadelphia Board of Education hearing concerning the needs of Spanish-speaking children, largely Puerto Rican, living in the Kensington area of that city.

Narrator:

Mrs. Aponte, you testified that you would like to see a Spanish-speaking member on the Board of Education. Why?

Mrs. Aponte:

There is a matter of racial pride. It hurts seeing whites and blacks on the board and not seeing a Puerto Rican there. I am very much concerned about the education of Spanish-speaking children, the Puerto Rican, the Cuban, and others from Latin America who live in this city. Very little has been done in this area mainly because we do not have a voice on the Board of Education. Had we this voice, much more would have been accomplished. With a person on the board we would have more power to meet the educational needs of the Spanish-speaking child.

Narrator:

What are the special needs of the Spanish-speaking child?

Mrs. Aponte:

The language barrier is a great problem. There is already a bilingual program in the schools where the teachers speak both Spanish and English. This must be expanded. Not only do we need more Spanish-speaking teachers, but we also need more Spanish-speaking counselors and school officials, people that are sympathetic and understanding of the students. We also need community schools—schools that remain open after classes for other activities—where boys can play baseball and basketball, where the gym remains open, and where children can do their homework right in school.

Narrator:

Are you satisfied with the Spanish-speaking representation in other areas of government?

Mrs. Aponte:

President Nixon has formed a committee to deal with the Spanish-speaking peoples in America. The head of this committee is Spanish-speaking but not Puerto Rican. This is all right. But Puerto Ricans are the second largest group among Spanish-speaking peoples, and we feel the deputy, the one second to the head, should be a Puerto Rican, so that he would be able to relate to the Puerto Ricans in the various states. Also, federal programs available to other groups in various cities should also serve the needs of Puerto Ricans. At the present time we have little part in these programs.

Narrator:

Do you feel there is a greater need for Puerto Rican representation in Philadelphia government?

Mrs. Aponte:

Right! Let me give you an example. For several years the mayor of Philadelphia employed Mr. Pasqual Martines to act as a liaison between the city and the Puerto Rican community. He left about three years ago, and the mayor has never filled that position even though we have been asking him to do that.

Narrator:

If you could press a button and secure the solutions to your problems, have the necessary changes made, what areas would you want improved for the Spanish-speaking people?

Mrs. Aponte:

If I could press the button, I could see changes on the federal level where programs now available to others would be available to Spanish-speaking people, yet more of them and on a larger scale. Our people need more skills, and training programs which would teach them these skills. Men and women could attend classes in English and receive some income while doing so. Industrial firms could hire bilingual workers who would train the Spanish-speaking workers right on the job. We also need better housing programs to provide new apartments, renovation of present homes, and enforcement of housing codes so that renters have decent living quarters.

I have talked about schools: more bilingual programs, teachers, and counsellors. Yet even the hospitals in this community are not equipped to serve Spanish-speaking people. They need bilingual personnel. Patients now need to bring their own interpreter. The signs in the hospital clinics say if you cannot speak English, you must bring an interpreter.

Narrator:

Thank you very much for this interview, Mrs. Aponte.

Mrs. Aponte:

You are welcome.

How Do Minority Ethnic-Group Members Obtain Political Office?

RELIGION AND ETHNICITY IN CONGRESS 1977

Group	Members in Congress	Church membership
Roman Catholic	132	48,390,990
Jewish	33	5,870,000
Protestant Groups (selected)		
Methodist	86	10,671,774
Baptist	57	27,588,478
Presbyterian	54	3,087,213
Episcopal	64	3,285,826
blacks	17	22,580,289
women (sex group)	17	51% of U.S. 210 million

U.S. Congress: 535 members

Source: *Congressional Quarterly, Weekly Report,* January 1, 1977.

What does the above chart say about the relationship of selected ethnic groups and representation in Congress? While immigrants, religious groups, and racial minorities, for the most part, dress, act, and accept American ways, that is, "acculturate," they are not completely integrated into all areas of American life. In the world of politics nonwhite Protestant minorities remain underrepresented in government, particularly at the higher levels as the above chart indicates. Complete political assimilation will occur if such

200

minorities would hold office in the same proportion as their percentage of the population.

We have learned that certain groups feel that they can get things done for their fellow members if they have representatives in political office. How do they get in? In the previous activity you learned about ticket balancing—the fine art of maintaining a fair distribution of offices among ethnic groups on party-endorsed slates of candidates—as one way of integration. This learning activity offers another. It focuses on three political figures: Vito Marcantonio, an Italian American who served as a congressman for 16 years until 1949; Congresswoman Shirley Chisholm, a black lady still representing the Bedford-Stuyvesant section of Brooklyn, New York; the third is the first Puerto Rican to serve in Congress, Herman Badillo, elected in 1970. The data on him is a blurb from the *Congressional Directory,* which gives you an idea where one gets information on representatives. All three came out of districts where there were heavy concentrations of their fellow ethnics.

In the short biographies some attention is paid to their personal lives. What kind of people make successful politicians? A clue can be taken from your own school. Examine the records of the past few presidents of your school's elective body. The information is readily found in the school yearbook. List the steps by which they won this office. Is there a pattern? If so, perhaps this pattern will hold for candidates in the area of ethnic politics.

When you have completed listing the steps which helped students to become presidents, read the biographical accounts that follow. As you read:

1. Determine to what extent they followed steps similar to, or different from, the steps followed by your school president.

2. Determine the role of ethnicity—identification with an ethnic group, support by the ethnic group and by ethnic organizations—in their careers.

3. Check your explanation against political analyst Samuel Lubell's description of patterns he has observed on how ethnic minorities win office. Lubell uses the term *minority* to mean an ethnic group that has been handicapped by its lack of political, social, and economic power. Note Lubell's sequence in his "ladder." Do you agree with his conclusion?

The Special Case of Vito Marcantonio

Ethnic influences constituted a major part of Marcantonio's youth. His mother and grandfather were immigrants, his friends were Italian, his heroes were Italian, and his home was in the most Italian neighborhood in the United States. Like LaGuardia, he spoke Italian, ate Italian food, and regaled in Italian customs. As a young high school student, he showed deep concern for promoting Italian-American causes. Thus, he joined with other Italo-Americans in high school, and became the founder and leader of Circolo Italiano, an organization designed to stimulate interest in Italian culture, while simultaneously working for Italian assimilation in the American social fabric. He continued his interest in Italian clubs in college, becoming president of Circolo Mazzini at New York University, and continuing as an enthusiast for the formation of an interscholastic organization of Italian clubs. So thorough was his ethnic identification, that he often performed in Italian plays while in school. As part of his extra-curricular activity, he became a citizenship education teacher in a project aimed at preparing Italian immigrants for active and responsible citizenship. When, on one occasion LaGuardia visited his high school in his capacity as President of the Board of Aldermen, Marcantonio was selected as the student speaker of the day because of his ethnic background.

As a LaGuardia protege, Marcantonio managed the Fiorello H. LaGuardia Political Association, which brought together a cross-section of Italians interested in promoting the political aspirations of their ethnic brothers. He was entrusted with the task of serving as LaGuardia's "eyes and ears" in East Harlem, a job which included a great amount of work in dealing with Italian constituents. Displaying uncommon zeal as LaGuardia's campaign manager, he mobilized Italo-Americans in support of LaGuardia's candidacy, making the LaGuardia Association the most effective political

Excerpted and reprinted by permission from Salvatore J. LaGumina, "Case Studies of Ethnicity and Italo-American Politicians," in *The Italian Experience in the United States,* ed. Silvano M. Tomasi and Madeline H. Engel (Staten Island, New York: Center for Migration Studies, 1970), pp. 152–154, 159.

machine in the city. When LaGuardia ran for mayor in 1933, Marcantonio, although no longer his campaign manager, played a significant role by energetically and effectively circulating nominating petitions in Italo-American neighborhoods throughout the city. It was the virtually unanimous support of this ethnic group, cutting across party lines, which was largely responsible for electing New York's first Italo-American mayor. To Marcantonio, LaGuardia's election was a necessary step to achieve political justice for the Italians of East Harlem. Moreover, it would demonstrate conclusively that Italians had passed the stage of factionalism, the result of a provincial attachment to regionalism, which had prevented unification earlier.

When Marcantonio ran for Congress, he exploited his ethnicity to the fullest. Although his opponent was also an Italo-American, Marcantonio boasted of the endorsement from dozens of local Italian organizations and individuals, especially that of LaGuardia. With the possible exception of LaGuardia, no other Italo-American worked as indefatigably in the halls of Congress, with a substantial amount of his efforts directed toward the advancement of Italo-American interests. During his first term, he emerged as the foremost Congressional defender of aliens and immigrants against the backdrop of a huge anti-alien drive then under way. Intense interest in immigration restriction had become intertwined with pressing economic questions by the middle of the 1930's. Indeed, that decade spawned some of the nation's severest restriction bills, some of which gained approval, while others failed in large part because of the strenuous opposition led by men like Marcantonio.

A study of Marcantonio's activities in behalf of Italy and Italo-Americans during the war years is quite revealing. Often the subject of controversy because of his left-wing politics, and duly criticized for the same by many respected Italo-American leaders, nevertheless, when it came to the defense of the Italians, Marcantonio was second to none. On Capitol Hill, where policies affecting them were determined, he emerged as their leading champion. He was the first to call for a recognition of Italy, for its inclusion in the United Nations. He argued against imposing reparations on Italy, and prodded Administration officials to increase daily rations in the occupied country.

A committed left-winger, Marcantonio was not above urging political preference on the basis of ethnic identity. In 1943, for example, as leader of the left wing of the American Labor Party, then reigning as New York State's powerful third party, he obtained ALP support for Democrat Judge Thomas Aurelio for a Supreme Court judgeship, largely because of his insistence that the post go to an Italo-American.

Shirley Chisholm: Tempest on Capitol Hill

Congresswoman Shirley Chisholm's constituents in the poverty-stricken Bedford-Stuyvesant section of Brooklyn, New York, regard her as a ray of hope in a Congress they feel has given too low a priority to their pressing needs. Not so the entrenched, aging, conservative leaders in the House of Representatives. They take a less sanguine view of the tempestuous lady politician—the first woman of her race to serve in Congress—regarding her as a black plague that threatens some of their most cherished prerogatives.

In the tradition-bound halls of Congress, it is the rule that freshman members shall be seen and not heard until they have been indoctrinated with all of that body's crusty rules and formalities. These require, among other things, that an adversary be addressed as "my good friend and colleague, the distinguished gentleman from so-and-so," before you spit in his face. Mrs. Chisholm made it clear, almost from the moment she took her place in the marble chamber of the House, that respectful silence was not to be one of her endearing virtues. She lost no time disavowing any intention of being seen and not heard.

"They're going to hear from *me,*" she announced to the newsmen who keep watch on Capitol Hill. "Congress is badly in need of reform and I'm going to fight for this. We must change our priorities."

Reprinted by permission from Phillip Drotning and Wesley W. Smith, *Up from the Ghetto* (New York: Washington Square Press, 1971), pp. 112–119.

Congresswoman Shirley Chisholm by Capitol in Washington, D.C. Courtesy Wide World Photos.

Then, uncorking a bare-knuckled blow at the power structure in the House of Representatives, she added:

"It is shocking to me that there are so many old men with such power over the destiny of the country who are so much out of touch, out of tune, with the country. It's just shocking. Maybe I was expecting too much. The seniority system is horrible. The experience of people is important, but in a dynamic country like this, it is not right to reward people just for length of service.

"People have to have creativity and fresh outlooks about problems. The thing that happens to a lot of old men is that they are not attuned to what's happening. There must be a way to make more use of younger members with capacity and talent to help lead this country. We must open the doors of leadership to congressmen and congresswomen with something more to give than mere longevity of service. Men of experience are necessary, but so are men of real ability.

"We are in bad shape in this country, and I believe one of the reasons is that we are running the country by traditional rules that are obsolescent for today's needs."

The occasion for Mrs. Chisholm's maiden outburst was the

announcement of the House leadership that she had been assigned a seat on the Agriculture committee. Since any farming done in her congested urban district would have to take place on a forty-foot lot, she regarded the assignment at best as an affront and at worst as an attempt to isolate her on a committee with the least possible relevance to her interests and her constituency—a vineyard in which her militance would have little chance to flower.

"Apparently all they know here in Washington about Brooklyn is that a tree grew there," the black congresswoman said. "I can think of no other reason for assigning me to the House Agriculture committee."

Mrs. Chisholm, a slightly built 105-pound bundle of energy, characterizes herself as "a firm, tough woman," and she proved it in her initial encounter. She challenged the House leadership before the Democratic caucus and won. They took her off the committee on Agriculture and put her on the Veterans committee. She would have preferred Education and Labor, but at least her present assignment has relevance to the concerns of many people in her district, and in forcing the change she had made her point.

Victims of Mrs. Chisholm's wrath seeking to place the blame for her unrelenting and sometimes abrasive determination can look to her imposing, six-foot-three-inch grandmother, who raised Shirley when she was a small child. Although she and her three sisters were born in Brooklyn, their parents took them to Barbados when Shirley was three, and they lived there with their grandmother until the child was ten years old.

Her parents returned to the United States with the objective of working as hard as they could and saving money that would enable them to give their children "a very good education."

"This was always uppermost in the minds of my parents," Mrs. Chisholm says. "Since they did not have a formal education they felt it was very important, that education was the key to everything. They vowed that if nothing else they were going to give their daughters a good education. My mother would put by even two or three cents at a time against the day we would enroll in college. In the end, however, three of us got scholarships and paid our own way, and my parents were able to take the money they had saved and buy a house."

Shirley's grandmother was a very stern and demanding woman who imposed the strictest discipline on the children, and early taught them a sense of responsibility to themselves and to others.

"She gave me the philosophy that made me a strong woman," Mrs. Chisholm says. "She always used to say you must have courage and conviction and remember that, when you take a stand on things in this world, quite often you are going to find yourself alone. How often I have found that true in my own political experience. There have been so many times when I have had to stand alone, but I have the guts and the courage to do it because of what this wonderful old lady did for me as a child. She imprinted on my mind the necessity to fight for that in which you believe, even though you may not always have supporters."

Mrs. Chisholm is extremely grateful for the education she received in Barbados. She was reading at three and writing by the time she was four. She had a near-genius IQ, and when she returned to school in America she was well ahead of her peers, a circumstance which she attributes to the superior quality of instruction in the British school system.

"They had a more serious approach to education on the part of both children and teachers," she says. "They were more strict, permitted less freedom, and the result was better preparation of the student."

Shirley and her family lived for a time in the Brownsville area of Brooklyn and then moved to a home on Ralph Avenue in Bedford-Stuyvesant. At that time Brownsville was an integrated, primarily Jewish neighborhood, but Bedford-Stuyvesant was already predominantly black.

The family was very poor. Shirley's parents both worked when they could, her mother as a seamstress, and her father as an unskilled laborer in a burlap bag factory, where he sorted and packaged bags. Although Shirley was only eleven, her parents left her each day with a latchkey around her neck to care for her younger sisters. She took the younger girls to school in the morning, brought them home, and prepared their lunch, "and made sure that they ate it." The child was given a dime a week for her allowance, but didn't always get it because sometimes her parents just didn't have ten cents that they could spare.

"At one time during the Depression we were on welfare," Mrs. Chisholm recalls. "We would get an allotment of clothing each month. Mother always had trouble with me because I was so proud I refused to wear the welfare dresses to school. They were so obviously welfare that some of the other children would jeer. Sometimes mother had to whip me to get me to put on the dress and go to school."

Even in their darkest days, Mrs. Chisholm does not recall food as having been a problem. "Mother was a good cook," she says. "She could pick up the most unappetizing things and make a tasty meal of them, so that even though we were poor we never really did have a shortage of good food to eat because mother was so ingenious."

Despite their poverty, Mrs. Chisholm says she had "a wonderful childhood." She enjoyed school and feels that she received a good education in the New York schools. She adds, however, that this was before many of the current problems had developed, and she believes that a larger community role in the neighborhood schools is necessary if the current level of education in New York is to be improved.

Most of the congresswoman's unpleasant recollections are not related to the economic circumstances of the family, but to the indignities she suffered because of her race. A sensitive person, she was aware as a child that something was wrong around her. She began to sense that there was something different in the way teachers talked to black children, the way things were said, the way black children were handled.

"One time in Brownsville eleven neighborhood kids went to a ball game together," she recalls. "Four were Jewish kids and seven of us were black.

"As you know, children don't harbor racial discrimination. It is something they have to be taught. They play on their blocks together and have a good time until they are at an age when their parents begin to make them aware of the fact that some of them are white and the others are black.

"On this occasion we went to the ball game, laughing and happy together because for all of us it was a real treat. But when we got there and started to sit together the white kids were separated from us and put in another section, even though they didn't want to be. I'll never forget that. It was so humiliating that it sticks in my mind. I was only twelve at the time.

"When I got home I asked my parents about it, and all they would say was, 'You learn a lot when you get older.' They always had trouble explaining why blacks should be treated different from everyone else.

"Oh yes, I felt the reaction of white toward black at a very early age. That is why I fight the way I do, and why I am so intense about what I am doing."

Mrs. Chisholm attended a girls' high school in the heart of Bedford-Stuyvesant. She was such an exceptional student that she got "all kinds of grants and scholarships." She enrolled in Brooklyn College and got her degree in social work, and then went on to Columbia University to earn a master's degree and professional diploma in the field of early childhood education.

After her graduation from Brooklyn College, Shirley began applying for employment, but met with many rebuffs. She had graduated cum laude, spoke well, dressed well, and had poise and confidence. Yet repeatedly, when she applied for jobs in competition with white classmates who were her intellectual and scholastic inferiors, they were hired and she was not. This embittered her because she knew that she was being rejected because she was black.

"When I was at Brooklyn College and in the debating society my professor suggested that I had leadership and speaking ability and that I should enter politics," Mrs. Chisholm says. "I forgot about it because I felt that blacks, and especially black women, essentially didn't have a chance.

"After I came out of college and became involved in the educational world I began to feel that I had to become involved. I was so angered by many things, and not just those things that had happened to me. Increasingly, as a teacher, people kept asking me to represent them and to become involved in volunteer civic work. I finally decided that I would have to fight the system, even if I had to stand alone."

That was twenty years ago, and she has been involved in politics ever since. Mrs. Chisholm was encouraged by her husband,

Conrad, "a man who understood and understands me," and who saw in her a capacity for leadership. She, in turn, has also encouraged him.

Mr. Chisholm, when Shirley met him, was a waiter for the Horn and Hardart Company. Born in Jamaica, he was one of thirteen children of a village mayor. He had first come to the United States as a farm worker under the contract program, worked on farms in the Midwest, returned to Jamaica, and then was readmitted under an immigrant visa.

Mrs. Chisholm observed that her husband had an unusual faculty for remembering places and people, and encouraged him to enter the field of investigation and criminology. He enrolled in school, finished second in his class, and for nine years worked as a private detective. Then, two of his companions were killed while on duty, and Mrs. Chisholm became deeply concerned that her husband would meet a similar fate. She persuaded him to abandon his career as a detective, and he is now senior investigator for the New York City Department of Hospital Services.

Mrs. Chisholm was the first black woman elected to the New York State Assembly. She ran under the banner, "unbought and unbossed."

I can say that perhaps I am the only unbossed and unbought politician in Brooklyn," the congresswoman says. "I am in nobody's hip pocket and nobody gives me a lot of money to win an election. I probably ran the cheapest congressional election in this country this past year, and that money came from the people in my community."

Mrs. Chisholm says that any doubts she had about running for Congress were resolved early in the campaign when a man came to her door and handed her a crumpled envelope.

"Chisholm, this is the first," he said, and then disappeared.

Inside the envelope was $9.69, raised by people on welfare. Shirley cried a little over that contribution from people who could ill afford it, but before the campaign was over there were many more like it. The people in the community gave chitterlings parties, fashion shows, local teas, and resorted to every kind of fund-raising device to raise the twenty-eight thousand dollars that was spent in her behalf on both a hotly contested primary and a general election

Congressman Herman Badillo talks to people in his district. Why do ethnic groups want to see their members in public office? Courtesy Wide World Photos.

campaign against one of the outstanding figures in black leadership, James Farmer.

Mrs. Chisholm says she is "committed to nobody but the people."

Herman Badillo and the Twenty-First District*

TWENTY-FIRST DISTRICT.—That part of the county of Bronx bounded by a line described as follows: Beginning at a point where Manida Street extended intersects the waters of the East River, thence along said street extended and said street to Ryawa Avenue, to Coster Street, to Spofford Avenue, to Hunt's Point Avenue, to Lafayette Avenue, to Barretto Street, to Bruckner Boulevard, to Sound View Avenue, to Watson Avenue, to Bronx River Parkway,

Reprinted from *Official Congressional Directory,* 93rd Congress, First Session (Washington, D.C.: U.S. Government Printing Office, 1973), p. 129.

*Herman Badillo abandoned his Congressional seat which he held since 1970 to become deputy mayor of New York City on January 2, 1978.

to Cross-Bronx Expressway, to West Farms Road, to East Tremont Avenue, to Webster Avenue, to East 176th Street, to Park Avenue, to East 174th Street, to Washington Avenue, to East 173rd Street, to Park Avenue, to East 169th Street, to Webster Avenue, to East 168th Street, to Morris Avenue, to East 167th Street, to Sheridan Avenue, to McClellan Street, to Grand Boulevard and Concourse, to East 165th Street, to Walton Avenue, to East 161st Street, to River Avenue, to East 157th Street, thence westerly along said street and said street extended into the waters of the Harlem River, thence southerly and easterly through said waters and the waters of the East River to their intersection with Manida Street extended, the point of beginning, and including North Brother and South Brother Islands. Population (1970), 462,030.

HERMAN BADILLO, Democrat, of the Bronx, N.Y.; born in Caguas, P.R., August 21, 1929; first person of Puerto Rican birth to sit with a vote in the Congress of the United States; educated in the public schools and colleges of New York City; graduated from City College of New York as a Bachelor of Business Administration; majored in accounting and economics; graduated, cum laude, from Brooklyn Law School, 1954; class valedictorian, and on staff of Law Review; became Certified Public Accountant, 1956; in 1955 became a partner in the law firm of Permut & Badillo; in 1960, set up the John F. Kennedy Democratic Club in East Harlem; in 1962, appointed by Mayor Wagner commissioner of the newly created Department of Relocation; delegate to the Democratic National Convention, 1968 and 1972, and member of Credentials Committee; practiced law with the law firm of Stroock, Stroock & Lavan, 1969-; member of Rules Commission of Democratic National Committee (O'Hara Commission) since 1968; married Irma Deutsch, April 7, 1961; elected to 92d Congress November 3, 1970; reelected to the 93d Congress.

Jacob's Ladder

The key to the political progress of any minority element in this country would seem to lie in the success of the group's developing its own middle class. Sheer numbers alone are not enough for political power—witness the ineffectiveness so far of the Mexican-Americans of the Southwest. To be effective, numbers must be supported by economic, educational, and social progress.

Today college training or its equivalent is required for an increasing number of appointments. To register its political strength, a minority has to have its own lawyers or leaders with equivalent training. The more numerous middle-class members a climbing element has, the more demanding it becomes for political recognition.

Patronage, or the giving of political offices, to minority groups involves much more than a job for a minority member. Each first appointment given a member of any underdog element is a boost in that element's struggle for social acceptance. It means that another barrier to their advance has been lifted, another shut door has swung open. Whenever Franklin Roosevelt nominated a black to a white-collar post in the federal government, he transmitted a thrill to every young black who thought instinctively, "Maybe there's a place up there for me or my child."

The opening of these new opportunities, in turn, stimulated the political ambitions of the group, encouraging its leaders to eye the next highest post on the patronage ladder.

In most northern cities, the political parties have actually developed a ladderlike succession of posts, through which the political progress of various minority groups is recognized. First, just as one judges how far any minority has climbed economically by the kind of neighborhood where it dwells, so can one measure its effective political power by the kind of political offices its members have.

The earliest stirrings of any group usually are satisfied by an appointment as assistant district attorney (the lowest rung of the ladder ascending upwards). This entails little more than some mem-

Adapted from Samuel Lubell, *The Future of American Politics* (New York: Harper & Brothers, 1952), pp. 75–78.

bers of the group be educated as lawyers. A county judgeship, on the other hand, requires a candidate who has succeeded in a lower post, and has a large enough vote to withstand the competing claims of other minority groups of voters and the economic backing to finance a campaign. Similarly with elected posts, the solid vote of an ethnic element may win a council seat in city government, or a seat in the state legislature, or even a seat as congressman from a local district. But no minority group can be said to have "arrived" politically until its members can appeal beyond their ethnic boundaries to win a county or city-wide election; in other words, when the candidate can get other ethnic groups to vote for him so that he wins a major political post such as mayor.

The emphasis on hyphenated candidates—Polish-Americans, Italian-Americans, Afro-Americans, Hispanic-Americans—for balancing the slate is often condemned as "un-American." Those who do the condemning do not see ethnic groups as having group interests and believe (as if there were just one) that the "best man" should be chosen. Yet, putting the so-called "ethnic" candidates on the ballot is really a major move in the adjustment process, serving as a means by which minority elements are absorbed into the structure of government.

THEME TWELVE

Important Public Issues Grow Out of Ethnic Political Behavior

Rabbi Meir Kahane and others of the Jewish Defense League were arrested outside the Soviet Embassy after protesting violations of human rights in the Soviet Union. See pages 235–237. Courtesy the *Philadelphia Inquirer*.

On What Issues Do Ethnic Groups Express Themselves?

Part I. Foreign Affairs

Ethnically conscious Americans are interested in what happens to their mother country, the country from which an ethnic group emigrated, or to the people from which they descend, who may not always have a nation of their own. Even though their grandparents or great-grandparents may have left the mother country years ago, members of ethnic groups can be excited by a foreign-affairs issue concerning brethren overseas, so excited that they change their voting patterns to support a different party or candidate than they normally would. Such concerns can also be cultural. Some Afro-Americans, in fact, after a long period of indifference, have been turning to black Africa as a source of cultural identity.

For this learning experience you will read three different selections. The first, digested from a book, traces political attitudes and voting patterns of a group—German-Americans—at the time of World War I (1914–1918). United States policy led by President Woodrow Wilson was pro-British and anti-German. The next selection, taken from a newspaper, concerns an American ethnic group whose ancestoral homeland has been under Soviet rule since 1939. The last article deals with a black parallel institution which you read about earlier. This vocational training school has had great success in educating and placing blacks into responsible jobs.

As you read, consider: (1) What do the three groups have in common? (2) What relationship exists between ethnic awareness in the United States and concern by an ethnic group about American policy involving brethren outside our borders? (3) Are any of these groups less American for their concern? Why or why not?

President Woodrow Wilson waves to crowd in Los Angeles as he promotes ratification of the peace treaty after World War I. Courtesy the Library of Congress.

The German-Americans and President Woodrow Wilson

The ethnics were very much concerned with the outcome of the First World War, since the homelands of so many of them were involved.* The war itself, and then the peace which followed, became important political issues, particularly in the elections of 1918 and 1920. And President Woodrow Wilson, as the leading American figure in the War and the peace, became himself a complex issue as a symbol of many things.

No Chicago ethnic group was as involved in these issues as were the German-Americans. Their position, especially after the United States joined the Allies [in 1917], was very difficult, and their interest was very great. As early as 1916 most German-

Adapted from John M. Allswang, *A House for All Peoples* (Lexington: University of Kentucky Press, 1971), pp. 112–115.

*Allswang uses the term "ethnic" to mean the immigrant generation and their children.

Americans considered Wilson pro-British, and preferred the election of Charles Evans Hughes to the presidency. Up until the time that the United States entered the war, the *Abendpost,* like the rest of the German-language press, continued to justify the German cause; indeed, the *Abendpost* charged the United States with responsibility for the rupture of diplomatic relations [with Germany] in early 1917.

Once America entered the war, however, the *Abendpost* became very patriotic and pro-Wilson, for reasons of self-preservation as well as sincere patriotism. This [patriotism] was facilitated by the issuance of the Fourteen Points in early 1918, which the *Abendpost* accepted with great enthusiasm and which was the keystone of its support of the Democrats in the fall elections. President Wilson was a "man of peace," the paper said, who had gone to war "only against the German government, not against the German people," and who wanted a League of Nations "of all people," including the Germans. For this reason, all of "Wilson's personal candidates" should be elected. . . . James Hamilton Lewis, campaigning for re-election to the Senate, played up this idea of a "just peace," and added that Berlin is looking "to Illinois—this Illinois, the largest German state of America." The *Abendpost* supported Lewis, and so did German-American voters. Traditionally Republican, they gave Democrat Lewis 54 percent of their senatorial vote.

But the German-Americans were very strongly anti-League of Nations by 1920. The peace treaty with Germany was far different than they expected, being exceedingly harsh in their eyes. The proposed League excluded Germany, and they felt Wilson had gone back on his promises. Throughout the nation the German-language press rebuked "Wilsonism" in strong language and hoped for the nomination of isolationist Hiram Johnson by the Republicans for the presidency. The German-Americans ultimately supported the Republican Warren Harding as the anti-Wilson presidential candidate in the 1920 elections.

Simas Kudirka speaking before an American audience after the Soviet Union eventually allowed him to settle in the United States. Courtesy ELTA.

Lithuanian Seaman Not Forgotten by Community

by Michael von Moshzisker

Defection means desertion and implies that the defector has breached or abandoned a loyalty he once owed to the country from which he defected. Applying the term to Simas Kudirka, the seaman who sought sanctuary aboard a United States Coast Guard cutter and was brutally returned to his Soviet masters, is unfortunate. Kudirka owed not a speck of loyalty to Soviet Russia. Instead he was—and is, if he still lives—a Lithuanian, entitled to be proud of an ancient national heritage. Subject to Russia, Kudirka may have been—but involuntary, as in the case of other Lithuanian citizens; the land of the hammer and sickle had no more claim to the young seaman's

Adapted from the *Philadelphia Bulletin,* December 31, 1970.

loyalty than we have to that of the captured Vietnamese. Fealty cannot be based on chains or allegiance on power alone.

This was made clear during an evening which my family and I spent in the company of Stanley A. Gecys and Mrs. Austra M. Zerr, the former an engineer with the Budd Company, the latter a Wyndmoor housewife. Both are leaders of Philadelphia's Lithuanian community.

Lithuania, you see, was established as a kingdom more than 700 years ago (1251 A.D.), and has rightfully been an independent country. The Russian rulers, the czars, did conquer the nation, but Lithuania's independence returned on February 16, 1918. A peace treaty with Soviet Russia followed. Just before World War II, the Soviet Union swallowed up the tiny nation along with Latvia and Estonia; however, the Lithuanians still have an embassy in Washington, D.C., recognized as an independent nation by the United States.

In 1863, Lithuania and Poland rose against the Russian czar—but unsuccessfully. And so it was that refugees emigrated to this country and founded Philadelphia's Lithuanian community, much as my own grandfather came here after fighting with the Polish patriot Kossuth for a free Poland in 1848.

Today, there are three Lithuanian parishes here: St. Casimer's in South Philadelphia, St. Andrew's at 19th and Wallace Streets, and St. George's on Venango Street in Richmond. Two of these have parochial schools, and the third—St. Andrew's—maintains a school where on Saturdays, persons of Lithuanian descent come with their children to study their native language, traditions, customs and dances.

Is this good? I am convinced that it is. Whites, like blacks, can find inner strength that comes from one's ethnic heritage, a source of pride which need not be lost in the melting pot.

We should be glad, then, that the sad affair of seaman Simas Kudirka was greeted responsibly by this city's Lithuanian-Americans. They protested to the President of the United States, to the Vice-President, to the Transportation Department which has control over the offending Coast Guard, and—through the good offices of Congressman Eilberg—to the Secretary of State. Then they demonstrated in front of the Coast Guard recruiting station on

North Broad Street. Kudirka, dead or alive, has not been forgotten by these good people.* If they do little to help him, still their forthright protests nevertheless reflect honor on Philadelphia's Lithuanian community, and may help prevent future injustice.

Rev. Sullivan Plans More OICs in Africa

by Rem Rieder
Bulletin Washington Bureau

Washington, D.C. Opportunities Industrialization Center, the Philadelphia-based group which has set up self-help centers in 90 American cities, is seeking a massive expansion of its African operations.

The Rev. Leon H. Sullivan, OIC's founder, got together with representatives of 26 African nations—19 of them ambassadors—yesterday to discuss the idea over lunch.

Yesterday's luncheon at the Ghana Embassy provided an opportunity for Mr. Sullivan to express his plans. Besides its economic benefits the pastor of the Zion Baptist Church said, the exporting of his job-training program to Africa would have great symbolic significance.

"We have never seen anything like this before: A program started by black Americans set up in black Africa."

Thus far most of the financial backing for OIC's African endeavors started last week in Ghana and Nigeria has been provided by the United States Agency for International Development (AID), which has put up $1.7 million. Rev. Sullivan would like to see the ante upped to $40 million.

"This is a giant step in United States' help for Africa. It's self-help, not control." Sullivan said that he has received $25 mil-

Adapted from the *Philadelphia Bulletin,* February 11, 1971.

*Seaman Simas Kudirka was permitted to leave Soviet Lithuania and emigrate to the United States, where he is now a permanent resident. [Author]

lion for the OIC's program in the United States so far. "I have great support at the White House," he explained.

While OIC has concentrated primarily on preparing people for jobs, it has also engaged in some economic development plans, like shopping centers and, in one instance, an aerospace plant.

"If America can support Israel for the Jews," the founder of the Opportunities Industrialization Center concluded, "It can support Africa for the Africans."

On What Issues Do Ethnic Groups Express Themselves?

Part II. Domestic Issues

Political issues affect ethnic behavior and vice versa. The preceding lesson touched on foreign affairs. This lesson looks at a major issue that relates to our second largest religious group, American Catholics. While other religious denominations maintain private schools, Catholics have the largest parochial school system. Their schools are now suffering from a critical shortage of money and need outside funds for support. The issue of public support of private religious schools has raised a constitutional question: Would such funds be supporting a religion and thus violate the intent of the First Amendment of the Constitution of the United States?

This issue has raised the larger question of the role of government toward the many ethnic groups that make up America. Some see the public school as an assimilating agency. Just as the body digests food, changing it to a form that is absorbed by all parts of the body, so, too, do believers in the *melting pot* idea see a similar process for the diverse groups that make up America. *Assimilationists* would like to see Americans shed their differences and blend into a common culture, uniquely American. *Pluralists,* on the other hand, believe that ethnic differences are a positive good, and they wish to preserve and strengthen ethnic subsocieties. Recently the pluralists, at least in education, received a setback, for the Supreme Court of the United States ruled that states may not give money directly to religious schools.

The information following focuses on the issue of public support for religious schools. *Read the various opinions given and determine what kind of argument is offered—constitutional, pluralist, assimilationist, or some combination. Be ready to describe this argument. How does religious belief influence the thinking of many people on this issue?*

The Majority Opinion of the Supreme Court on State Aid to Parochial Schools*

The sole question is whether state aid to parochial schools can be squared with the dictates of the religious clauses of the Constitution. Under our system the choice has been made that government is to be entirely excluded from the affairs of religion.

The Constitution decrees that religion must be a private matter for the individual, the family, and the institutions of private choice, and that while some entanglement with government is inevitable, lines must be drawn. This case introduces the hazards of religion intruding into the political area. . . . The Pennsylvania law under question will cause excessive entanglement of government and religion.

Believers in parochial schools understandably concerned with rising costs will campaign for more state funds to their schools and promote political action to achieve their goals. Those who oppose state aid whether for constitutional, religious, or financial reasons will inevitably respond and employ the usual campaign techniques. Candidates will be forced to declare and voters to choose. It would be unrealistic to ignore the fact that many people faced with issues of this kind would vote according to their religious faith.

Ordinary political debate and division, however vigorous, are normal and healthy expressions of our democratic system of government, but political division along religious lines was one of the

Edited from the Supreme Court decision *Lemon* v. *Kurtzman,* 1971, by the author.

*The Supreme Court has the power under the Constitution to determine, when a case is brought before it, whether a law of a state is constitutional or not. Eight justices, with no opposition, ruled that a Pennsylvania law which had the state reimburse nonpublic schools for such services as textbooks and teachers' salaries was in violation of the First Amendment.

principal evils against which the First Amendment of the Constitution was intended to protect. Such a conflict along religious lines is a threat to the normal political process.

"Court Denies Rights of Parents"

The following is the full text of a statement by John Cardinal Krol, fifteen other Roman Catholic bishops in Pennsylvania and three Ukrainian prelates, on the financial crisis in the parochial school system:

The Constitution of the United States guarantees religious and political liberty to every citizen. Precisely for this reason, we, the Catholic Bishops of Pennsylvania, feel compelled to speak to our fellow citizens about certain implications of the recent United States Supreme Court decision relating to non-public elementary and secondary education. Our purpose is not to discuss the particular programs upon which the Court saw fit to rule, nor indeed the related tax and educational crisis affecting every citizen in our commonwealth. Rather we address ourselves to the features of the decision which affect the basic freedoms of all. These freedoms relate to parental rights, the free exercise of religion, and the liberty of every citizen to speak, assemble, petition and vote.

The fundamental right of parents to educate their children in schools of their religious choice has often been challenged by secularists.[1] This right is guaranteed by our Constitution and was recognized a half century ago in the Pierce case[2] wherein the Supreme Court said:

"The child is not the mere creature of the state." But today the

Reprinted by permission of the *Philadelphia Inquirer*, August 12, 1971.

[1]Secularists believe that public education and other matters of government should be conducted without the introduction of the religious element. [Author]

[2]In the *Pierce* v. *Society of Sisters* case (1925) the Court ruled an Oregon law requiring every child to attend *public school* was unconstitutional. [Author]

highest court of the land—dealing with a case intimately related to parents—makes no mention of that right. Instead, its decision ominously points to a state educational monopoly in which parental rights—if acknowledged at all—will be exercisable only by the wealthy, by those who can bear the burden of school taxes and of the separate added cost of non-public schooling.

Today the effects of taxation, inflation and rising governmental costs make it growingly impossible for parents to exercise their Constitutional freedom without enabling assistance. The Commonwealth of Pennsylvania, through its successful program of the past three years of aid to non-public education, has recognized government's obligation in justice to make accommodation necessary to secure parental rights in education. It affirmed that, for parents to exercise this right today, they need and are entitled to a measure of economic help—a share of the tax dollars they pay.

We are hopeful and confident that the Commonwealth will promptly enact new legislation which, whatever its form, will come to the aid of Pennsylvania parents in the exercise of their rights.

Furthermore, we call upon the Supreme Court to use its vast powers in appropriate cases to emphasize parental rights in education and to repudiate every effort to make the child "a mere creature of the state."

The Supreme Court, in its decision, has warned that questions of state aid to church-related education must be kept out of the public forum because they present "hazards of religion intruding into the political area." This warning must be rejected.

There can be no political liberty in a society in which religious groups and individual believers, as such, may not speak out on public issues. There can be no religious liberty in a society in which public issues may not be discussed in their religious dimension.

The Supreme Court has also stated that "religion must be a private matter for the individual, the family and the institutions of private choice." Religion is indeed a private matter, but it is far more than that. Since the founding of the Commonwealth, it has been deemed, in an important sense, a very public matter. The separation of church and state is a wise policy. The separation of religion from public life is dangerous folly.

The totalitarian states of the present day[3] boast of their insistence that "religion must be a private matter." This is one reason why they are totalitarian. We Americans have always known that religious liberty is inseparable from its public expression.

We trust that citizens concerned over parental rights, religious liberty, diversity and excellence in education, and the avoidance of the increased taxation resulting from a state monopoly of education will now work, peaceably and with renewed vigor, for useful programs of aid to the education of all children.

We trust that religious-minded citizens of all faiths will continue to bear witness to the truths they hold, so that—as always before in American history—religion will help guide the destiny of our great nation.

Selection 1

"Parental Rights" Still Stand in the Choice of Schooling

On the opposite editorial page today we are publishing the full text of a statement by the Catholic bishops of Pennsylvania "about certain implications of the recent United States Supreme Court decision relating to non-public elementary and secondary education."

We do so with full respect for the views of this distinguished group of churchmen. We do not, however, agree with them.

On the contrary, we believe that they are misreading the court decision.

[3]Governments such as communist China or the Soviet Union which seek to control its people from the cradle to the grave tolerate no differing opinions from the policies set by the leaders. [Author]

Editorial of June 29, 1971; reprinted by permission of the *Philadel-*
the *Philadelphia Inquirer*.

To say that it is "the fundamental right of persons to educate their children in schools of their religious choice" is not to say that it was challenged in the cases recently before the Supreme Court, and we see nothing ominous in the court's failure to address this question directly.

On the contrary, the court accepted that right implicitly and discussed the existence of such schools matter-of-factly. And it carefully defined the limits of the question it was declining.

"The merits and benefits of these schools are not the issue before us in these cases," the court said. "The sole question is whether the state aid to these schools can be squared with the dictates of the religion clauses."

The court's answer was that it cannot, and we agree.

It does not follow from that, however, that "parental rights" are threatened in any legal sense.

Economically, it is undoubtedly true that the rising "burden of school taxes and of the separate added cost of non-public schooling," to use the bishops' phrase, makes it increasingly difficult for some parents to exercise that right.

The court's recent decision has clear pocketbook consequences—as indicated by the announcement Tuesday that Catholic elementary schools in the Philadelphia area will begin charging tuition for the first time this year and high school tuition will rise from $170 to $300 a year.

But financial hardship cannot justify the breach of the Constitutional principle of church-state separation which has served this nation well throughout its history.

Nor can the answer to the preservation of what the bishops call "*non-public* schooling" be found in turning to the public treasury for support. For then—as the self-contradictory terms suggest—the schools lose their non-public character and indeed their reason to exist.

The right to non-public schooling stands—as indeed it should. We recognize the place and value of such education in our pluralistic system. But the extent to which that right is exercised must continue to depend, as it has historically, on the depth of the commitment of those who prefer private or parochial schools which are open to all.

Selection 2

To the Editor:

I am a Nazareth Academy junior and I am very disturbed over the court ruling to abolish aid to non-public schools. Our government is built on a system of separation of church and state, but our government declares it is also a government for the people. How could it be? This ruling discriminates against our Catholic population.

The schools in the parochial system depended on $4.5 million to educate nearly half* the children of elementary age in Philadelphia.

LOUISE WALLOWICZ
Philadelphia

Reprinted by permission of the *Philadelphia Inquirer,* August 10, 1971.

*School census figures show one-third of the elementary children are in the parochial schools. [Author]

Selection 3

Comment to a Radio Talk Show

Giving money to the parochial schools would destroy the public-school system. What starts out as a crack becomes a hole and ends up as a canyon. Once the principle of the wall of separation between church and state is breached, there will be no end to the giving of public funds to private agencies. Other religious denominations would open schools. With a base in public funds middle-class parents will send their children to private religious schools and supply a little extra money to improve them. Right now they keep their children in public schools because private schooling is too expensive. If we ignore the Constitution, the public schools will become the repository of the poor and the minority groups.

Selection 4

To the Editor:

America grew strong because people of all beliefs, races, and nationalities joined in the common task of solving problems that confronted this nation. In fact the greater the diversity in the backgrounds of the people who are trying to solve a problem, the richer the imaginative pool from which creative solutions can spring to light.

How much more meaningful would be the solution to the parochial school problem if the people of good will from all segments of the religious spectrum joined in brainstorming sessions to define the problem and propose mechanisms to solve it.

George J. Beichl
Professor, St. Joseph's College
Philadelphia

Adapted from the *Philadelphia Bulletin,* February 11, 1971.

How Can We Identify and Analyze Ethnic Political Issues?

This activity should help you review the ideas and information studied in previous readings on ethnic politics. Most of the selections consist of adapted articles from newspapers. The first set of news items illustrates how politicians appeal to needs of various ethnic groups. *Tell to which group the politician is appealing and why the political pitch has an appeal for that ethnic group.*

The second set of items deals with the political behavior of blacks. *Identify the motives behind the behavior described in each. To what extent are blacks following traditional ethnic politics?*

The last selection is an editorial from a well-read large-city newspaper dealing with a Jewish demonstration. To examine the editorial it would be well to remember some terms. An *assimilationist* is one who does not like ethnic diversity and prefers to see the shedding of ethnic differences for a common core culture, one American set of ways of doing things. *Pluralists* favor ethnic group solidarity and are sympathetic to ethnic activity. *Assumptions* are beliefs or theories about what is or ought to be. Your task will be to (1) analyze the assumptions and position taken by the editorialist and (2) compose an answer that a participant in the Jewish demonstration might write as an answer to the editorial. Your teacher will give you a copy of an actual reply to which you may compare your answer.

A.   **Rep. Badillo Says U.S. Is Unfair
                           to Puerto Rico**

A stirring appeal to Congress to end discrimination against Puerto Rico in Federal programs was issued last month by Rep. Herman Badillo (D.-N.Y.): "The 2.7 million Puerto Ricans on the island of Puerto Rico and the 1.5 million in the United States represent one cohesive social and cultural body and community. We, in Congress, have a responsibility to meet the needs of all these—both on the mainland and on the island—and we must develop a coordinated and meaningful policy to deal with this community . . . ."

B.   **Hugh Scott Campaigns to Renew
                           His Senate Seat**

Old campaigner Senator Hugh Scott spoke at the Rhawnhurst Jewish Community Center. He stated that the security of Israel is essential to the security of the United States.

The Senator also spoke at the 30th anniversary celebration of the Ukrainian Congress Committee of America at the Benjamin Franklin Hotel. Scott commented that some of the nation's real concerns included disrespect for the forces of law and order, insane terrorist tactics of radicals, a need for more vocational education, and more dignity for the workingman as well as strong antipornography laws.

News items A, B, and C are based on actual events that are presented here by the author; D, E, F, and G are actual news items that appeared in the *Philadelphia Inquirer* and the *Philadelphia Evening Bulletin*.

C. Local Politician Supports Parents
in Battle of the Books

In past years there have been textbook battles between angry parents and school authorities, but none so intense as the one taking place in Charlestown, West Virginia. The parents, made up of white Anglo-Saxon, fundamentalist Protestants, in this coal mining area believe they should have a say in what their children read. They claim 350 new textbooks contain material that is "unChristian, unAmerican, dirty and obscene." They took exception to writings by Sigmund Freud, authors Dick Gregory and Eldridge Cleaver and poet Allen Ginsberg. Objectionable on the junior-high level were a collection of myths that challenged the literal interpretation of the Bible.

At least one politician has backed the parents and their striking mineworker supporters, claiming that educational authorities must be sensitive to the values of the community. He characterized the superintendent and his staff as "elitists who feel that the education of our young is too important to be influenced by parents." Referring to minorities whose sensibilities have been offended in the past, he reasoned that in this strict fundamentalist population, there should be concern for "the cultural values of this group and an input from the people whom the educational system serves."

D. What Happened to the Philadelphia Plan?

A program to increase the number of minorities in the skilled building trades was devised in Philadelphia under President Johnson and developed under the Nixon administration. Now Philadelphia black leaders are dissatisfied with the progress of the plan, which used Philadelphia as a model, for it has not appreciably boosted the meager 1.6 percent blacks in six building trades to a higher percentage. The original idea was that contractors who bid on federally assisted construction projects (such as public housing) were to make a "good-faith" effort to hire increasing percentages of minorities. But few blacks found jobs, which has discouraged Philadelphia leaders such as Clarence Farmer, the Human Relations Commission director, and Charles Bowser, head of the Urban Coalition. They charge the government with lax enforcement and failing to come up with a training program to increase the number of minority trainees. Bowser and other civil rights officials have gone to Washington eighteen times with no success to try to get funds for a program proposed by the Urban Coalition which would train minority journeymen for full entry into the skilled trades in a year or two.

E.   Black Caucus Asks Shapp to Appoint a Black

Delegates from the nine-member Black Caucus, black legislators in the General Assembly of Pennsylvania, the state's lawmaking branch, met with Governor Shapp. They demanded that he name a black to one of four new deputy-state-police-commissioner posts.

F.   Black Groups Seek Mayoral Prospect

A city-wide Black Political Convention will be held to draw up a slate of black candidates for the coming election. Groups initiating the move include: Council of Black Clergy, Congress of Racial Equality, Congress of African People and others.

G. **Negro Leaders Urge Black Unity at Polls**

Negro leaders met last night in an effort to form a united coalition aimed at improving conditions in black areas of the city. The meeting was attended by black leaders of 16 wards. The unity theme was sounded by Austin Norris, longtime Democratic leader, who stated, "The only solution for the black man is through the ballot box." He observed that while blacks as a group represented the largest segment of the population of the city, yet other groups, such as Irish, Italians, and Jews, "have greater representation."

They Don't Speak for America

The arrest of Rabbi Meir Kahane and 37 others Sunday, for demonstrating too near ("marching on") the Soviet Embassy, constrains us to observe once more that we have a State Department in this country which is responsible for making foreign policy and it should be allowed to do so.

Nobody elected Meir Kahane or his Jewish Defense League to determine what our relationship with the Soviet Union is to be. There is a nationally elected administration in office; if it doesn't perform to public satisfaction, it can be voted out.

But mobs in the street, or three or four youths over the fence of the embassy, give other Americans no voice or choice in the matter. They are being compromised in spite of themselves.

Many Americans will join Rabbi Kahane in believing that the Soviet Union is a "tyranny" and "stinks," but in a nuclear world the realities of power have to be faced.

World survival may well hang on the ability of the two greatest powers to coexist.

Editorial of June 29, 1971; reprinted by permission of the *Philadelphia Inquirer.*

We believe, with Jordan C. Band, former chairman of the Jewish Community Relations Council, that the foremost concerns of Jewish citizens, like those of other citizens, include "what is happening to our fresh air, our fresh water, with crime and poverty and drug abuse."

Albert E. Arent, just re-elected chairman of that national organization, said he was "disheartened" by a drift among some elements of the Jewish community to "group separatism" as already evidenced by the "so-called ethnics."

We deplore and deride the "inspired" marching by mobs in other countries—usually totalitarian—on our embassies; the ink bottles thrown at the walls, sometimes firebombs and brute violence. It never changes us except to arouse indignation.

It is no better, we submit, when crowds in our country threaten the embassies of others.

Legal Protests Are Desirable

To the Editor:

Your editorial of June 29, which quite properly condemns unlawful antics as a means of expressing grievances, seems to miss the mark about the role of protest in the American democratic process and the forming of American foreign policy.

It does not follow—as the *Inquirer* appears to suggest—that orderly, lawful demonstrations, even on a mass basis, also should be deplored. Expressing judgment on the shape of foreign policy should not be limited only to voting in national elections every two years as the *Inquirer* implies. (Parenthetically, it might be noted that indifference of the mass media to modest, orderly, responsible protest tends to encourage objectionable forms of protest.)

Of course, the State Department is responsible for making foreign policy—guiding the President would be more accurate. However, in the light of the "Pentagon Papers," it is questionable for the *Inquirer* to suggest that citizen groups should acquiesce except at elections in judgments of the State Department on American foreign policy. Furthermore, the now well-documented resis-

tance of the State Department officials to respond to the Nazi persecution of the Jews hardly encourages such confidence.

Apart from all this, the State Department itself issued a document this past February in which it asserted the great sensitivity of
the Soviet government to public outcries against its repression of
Soviet Jews. The State Department was explicit in encouraging
protests by private groups.

Men of conscience cannot be indifferent to the plight of 3
million Soviet Jews, as indeed, men of conscience should not be
indifferent in any manifestation of oppression. That protests on
behalf of Soviet Jewry will cause discomfort within government is
expected and desirable. This is reflected in limited positive Soviet
gestures. That it could conceivably lead to war as the *Inquirer*
implies is preposterous.

While men of conscience hopefully will respond, it would be
strange indeed for Jews not to be in the forefront in asserting the
aspirations of Soviet Jews. If Jews don't, who will? Asserting this
commitment of the Jewish community does not diminish our deep
concern about the need in this country for strong public educational
systems, fair and full employment, fair and full housing, and for the
redress of other critical problems searing the soul of American democracy.

Finally, the editorial fails to grasp the pluralistic character of
American society. It is the multiplicity of diverse groups and creeds
in competition, as one author has described it, that triggers America's vitality and creativity. The diversity of races, religions, and
creeds produces a great orchestration that is America's strength.

> Benjamin Loewenstein, President
> Jewish Community Relations Council
> of Greater Philadelphia

(Editor's note: The *Inquirer* did not suggest that "orderly, lawful
demonstration" to protest government policy should be deplored;
on the contrary, we have frequently defended such demonstration.
Our point was that in this instance the Jewish Defense League was
going beyond that and taking foreign policy into its own hands with
unlawful tactics—including scaling the fence in front of the Soviet
embassy in Washington—which brought the arrest of 34 people.)

Conclusion

Social scientists, like all scientists, hold their conclusions as tentative, that is, subject to change when new evidence is presented. In these concluding experiences you will have an opportunity to review and evaluate what you have learned. Topic 33 presents some negative evidence, conclusions of a sociologist who believes that social-class factors are most important in explaining behavior that this study feels is the result of ethnic factors. Like our study, he touches upon identity, neighborhood, organizational life, politics, and immigrant experiences. You will need your notes to compare and contrast what he says to the conclusions made throughout the unit. Your teacher has the names of other writers and their works which also support the social-class theory.

The last topic asks you to evaluate whether this study has achieved its objectives. In the preface its stated goals were to make you, the student, more aware of ethnicity, more self-conscious, more appreciative of the ethnicity of others, and more able to discern the social and political activity of ethnics. It also aimed at increasing an understanding of public issues by detecting ethnic factors and exploring and clarifying your views and values on a number of ethnic related issues. How well have the learning experiences done these?

Hopefully, you have gained by this study an insight into the nature of sociology, the study of human behavior in groups. You have been exposed to the kind of data that sociologists use—questionnaires, statistics, interviews, newspaper articles, and personal observation. You have been asked to think the way they think, by interpreting, analyzing, hypothesizing, and drawing conclusions. In no way has this study exhausted the field, even as a survey. You have been given a taste, a good taste. We hope you like what you have tried and seek out more.

THEME THIRTEEN

Ethnicity and the Role of Ethnic Groups Remain Controversial

Annual Columbus Day parade along New York City's Fifth Avenue. Do you think the observance of such occasions by ethnic groups reflects a genuine tie with their cultural and historical past, or is it only a middle-class gesture of descendants to their origins? Courtesy Wide World Photos.

Is Ethnicity the Answer?

In this study you have examined what amounts to an argument for the view that ethnicity, or membership in an ethnic group, constitutes a major factor explaining various kinds of behavior. Not all historians and social scientists agree with this hypothesis. Some believe that more important than one's membership in a racial, religious, or nationality group is one's membership in a social class. These scholars identify three large class divisions—upper, middle, and lower—and within each major division the subdivisions of upper and lower; hence there is an upper middle class and a lower middle class. They claim that each class has a particular set of characteristics—certain patterns of belief and behavior—and much of what is attributed to ethnic factors is really class-culture factors.

Edward C. Banfield, a Harvard professor of urban government and an author of a number of books on city politics, while not ignoring ethnic factors, stresses the class-culture hypothesis. The selection that follows has been adapted from his book *The Unheavenly City*. Examine what he says carefully and compare what you have learned in this unit to what he says about the following topics: neighborhood choice and neighborhood feeling, life-style of groups, organizational life, group politics, and the immigrant experience. *Where does this sociologist seem to agree or disagree with the ethnic interpretation of behavior in these areas? What does he suggest are the underlying sources of human behavior? What new questions do his assertions raise?*

Class Culture as an Explanation of Behavior

American sociologists usually define social class in terms of ''prestige'' or ''standing.'' An individual belongs to one or another class depending upon whether he is ''looked up to'' or ''looked down upon'' by the majority of the community. Most often income, education, family ties, occupation, and housing indicate this prestige or standing. It generally turns out that the people put in the same prestige class share the same outlook and style of life, a style learned in childhood, which serves as a lifestyle in adulthood. These prestige classes turn out to be subcultures, each having a unique set of characteristics. What I consider the most crucial, the defining characteristic, is the way each subculture provides for a more or less distant future. The more distant the future an individual can imagine, and for which he can discipline himself to make sacrifices, the ''higher'' is his class. For example, the individual who seeks more education and sacrifices his leisure time with the hope for a higher paying, more responsible job tends to be of a higher class.

This use of the word *class* differs from the ordinary one. As I use it, a poor, unschooled person of low status may be upper class if he is psychologically capable of providing for a distant future. By the same token, a rich member of society may be lower class if he cannot picture a future for himself or control his impulses, and lives from minute to minute.

The upper class and the middle class have much in common. Perhaps their characteristics can be understood best if contrasted with those of the working class, the ''blue-collar'' world. The upper- and middle-class individual has confidence in himself and his ability to shape the future, while the working-class person feels at the mercy of fate. The upper-class person worships education, personal growth for himself and his children, has tolerance of those who differ from him intellectually, encourages creativity, originality, and independence of mind. The middle-class person likes education, wants his children in college, but has less enthusiasm for non-conformity. The working-class person has less concern about

Adapted from Edward C. Banfield, *The Unheavenly City* (Boston: Little, Brown and Company, 1970), pp. 46–48, 56–58, 60–61.

Boston's North End has seen a succession of immigrants—Jews, the Irish, and now Italians—who enjoy the busy, crowded street life of the city. Courtesy Wide World Photos.

college, prefers practical training for a skill rather than a broad education. He wants his children to learn faith, respect for authority and obedience, rather than independence of mind.

There are differences among the classes in regard to living in neighborhoods. Unlike the upper-class member who likes privacy, quiet surroundings, and open space between him and others, the working-class member enjoys people around—a crowded neighborhood offers street life, excitement, and companions. However, the working-class individual has few deep friendships with his neighbors. He does like to know who they are, exchange words, and enjoys seeing and hearing their goings on. He is close to relatives, keeping his social visiting mainly with them.

The upper-class individual picks and chooses his neighborhood, desiring his friends and associates to share his values and interests. The middle-class individual also is fussy about location, but cannot afford to be exclusive. Like the upper class, he is bound more by sharing of interests than by bonds of kinship in his friendship patterns. The neighborhood does not have the same importance for the middle- and upper-class member as it does for the working class. The former sees the house and the neighborhood as a way station until he advances himself professionally. The working-class member is not going anywhere. His job is a dead end. He comes to feel protective about his neighborhood, desiring to keep it as it is, feeling that the streets, public accommodations, and neighbors are all part of "home," not just the house.

Inside the house working-class members adhere to a sharper distinction between the roles of men and women than middle-class families do. Middle-class husbands and wives are not as fussy about which sex should do household chores. They also tend to go together to outside activities, for the values of equality and togetherness play a large part in their thinking. On the other hand, working-class culture dictates that men have their jobs and interests and women have theirs.

Differences appear in organizational life, also. The higher-class member joins organizations to be of service, for causes, for ideals, frequently to promote the welfare of his community, city, or nation. The working-class member, when he joins an organization, does not do so to share a sense of high purpose, but rather for fun and companionship in activity. He has no wish to feel himself part of a community, except an ethnic one.

In regard to politics, the working-class member may vote, especially if someone asks him as a favor. His opinions on public matters stay on the beaten track; it does not occur to him to form opinions of his own. When he must choose between more and better community facilities on one hand and lower taxes on the other, the working-class individual chooses lower taxes. Unlike the classes above him, parks, libraries, and better schools mean little to him. However, he does not like a school to be a blackboard jungle, where students lack manners, respect, and discipline.

The higher-class individual wants to feel that his local government is honest, impartial, impersonal, and efficient. Unlike the higher-class person, motivated by political principles and issues, the working-class member votes according to ethnic and party loyalties, the appeal of personalities, and the hope of favors from party workers.

The class-culture theory makes sense in explaining the immigrants' experience. After 1840 immigration increased rapidly. The newcomers came from peasant cultures—first Irish, and then after

Columbia, Maryland, is one of America's new towns built on the desire for suburban living—space, privacy, and quiet. Courtesy Wide World Photos.

1885, southern Italian and eastern European—cultures more present-oriented than those from Great Britain and northern Europe. Coming from places where ordinary people never had opportunities to rise by effort and enterprise, these immigrants tended to believe in a world ruled by fate, and that only a miracle or great piece of luck could change their situation. The idea of self-improvement—and even more, that of community improvement—was unfamiliar

Even in cities such as this area of Watts in Los Angeles many working-class people desire to live in openness and parklike surroundings. Courtesy Wide World Photos.

and not understandable to them. They concerned themselves with survival, not progress; how to get food, drink, and shelter for the day preoccupied them. They came to this country less to improve their general condition than to escape starvation.

Among native Americans even the day laborer could read, write, and do simple arithmetic, but few among the peasant immigrants could. The immigrants from present-oriented cultures did not see the advantages of education and self-improvement generally. Even to some sympathetic observers it appeared that many of them would as soon live in hovels and broken-down houses as not. (Lower-class members do not find such conditions upsetting.) Unlike the native Americans and the more future-oriented immigrants from England and northern Europe, peasant immigrants seldom attended free libraries or took advantage of free schools. Very few became skilled workers, partly because of the prejudice of native-born employers against them, and partly because their present-oriented outlook and style did not suit the requirement of work and organization.

Eventually, however, all the immigrant groups succumbed to the native American ideal of future-mindedness. When they did, better jobs and advancement in all matters came also. Although they travelled at different rates of speed, all racial and ethnic groups headed in the same cultural direction—from less to more future-oriented.

STUDY GUIDE

CLASS AND ETHNIC EXPLANATIONS OF BEHAVIOR

Directions: Study carefully what Professor Banfield has to say about the following topics and compare his statements with what we have learned in this study. You may use your notes and materials gathered in the study. Come to a consensus in your committee in regard to each topic before the reporter prepares a ditto master for distribution to the class. Look for areas where Dr. Banfield and the evidence of the study AGREE and DISAGREE.

Topic: Neighborhood Choice and Neighborhood Feeling
Areas of Agreement

Areas of Disagreement

Topic: Life-style
Areas of Agreement

Areas of Disagreement

Topic: Organizational Life
Areas of Agreement

Areas of Disagreement

Topic: Group Politics
Areas of Agreement

Areas of Disagreement

Topic: Immigrant Experience
Areas of Agreement

Areas of Disagreement

TOPIC 34

Ethnic Identity and Ethnic Issues –
Where Do You Stand Now?

You have completed your study on the subject of ethnic groups and ethnicity, the expression of behavior of such groups and their role in American life. You have studied how the ethnic factor operates in self-identification, neighborhoods, organizations, and politics. At the beginning of the study you received questionnaires which were answered on the basis of your knowledge and thoughts at the time. Now that the conclusion is here, have you changed your mind on the questions of identity and issues raised by the opinion questionnaire? Also has this course accomplished its goals? This experience asks you to fill out some answers which indicate where you stand now. The first questionnaire contains evaluatory queries, and the second is the same opinion one you filled out before. Note the items where you have changed your mind and also where you have not changed. Be ready to discuss your views in class and defend them with evidence you gathered as a result of these weeks of study.

Some of you may find you are where you were in the beginning, but you should have an *educated opinion,* one that is supported by thought, developed reasons, and evidence to support your views.

REVISED QUESTIONNAIRE: WHERE DO I STAND NOW?

The purpose of this questionnaire, revised from the one found in Topic 1, is to determine whether you have changed to any degree in your feelings about your own identity. Try to answer each question as honestly as you can. The results will have nothing to do with your final grade. You may choose to add a remark or clarify your position on any question.

1. Encircle how strongly you identify with a religion or a particular sect (name) within that religion. (very strongly, fairly strongly, moderately, weakly, in name only)

2. Place the name of the national origins group of which you feel a part. (You may put mixed, give mixture, or no group.)

---

3. Encircle what interest you have in your national origins and religious group.
   National origins——great, moderate, little, none
   Religious——great, moderate, little, none

4. Would you say that this study has (heightened, lessened, had no effect) on your interest in your own ethnic group?

5. Would you say that this study has made your understanding of your parents' ethnic behavior (greater, less clear, not much different) than before?

6. Would you say that you now understand other groups (better, less clearly, about the same) as before?

7. Would you say that you are (more aware, as aware) of public issues with ethnic factors as before?

8. Would you say that you are (more clear, as clear, more confused) as to your opinions and values on ethnic-related decisions as before?

ATTITUDE QUESTIONNAIRE ON ETHNIC ISSUES*

date	name	section

Directions: This questionnaire seeks your opinions or beliefs and cannot fairly be recorded as part of your grades. Please answer with complete honesty. Place a check mark in the space provided next to the letter of the statement that comes closest to your view on each issue or topic. If no statement is acceptable, write in the space provided at D an original statement or reword a statement from A, B, or C which does express your view.

1. *Ethnic Neighborhoods*

_____A. Neighborhoods should be integrated with people of all different backgrounds to promote good intergroup relations and break down artificial divisions in American society.

_____B. Neighborhood preference is a matter of personal choice; clustering into neighborhoods by members of the same ethnic group is acceptable so long as there are no secret agreements to keep out members of other ethnic groups.

_____C. People are better off living in neighborhoods with their own kind; they feel comfortable and avoid interethnic conflict.

_____D. Other: _____

_____

_____

2. *"Foreign-Sounding" Names*

_____A. A person with such a name should change it to an American-sounding one; he or she is living in America now.

*Composed by Philip Rosen, instructor in history, Northeast High School, Philadelphia, PA, 1972.

_____B. Names are a means of identity; a person should not feel embarrassed if he or she keeps or changes his name.

_____C. A person should have pride in his or her name, for it is inherited as a birthright. If people have trouble in pronouncing or spelling the name, the person should take care to explain it to them.

_____D. Other: _____
_____
_____

3. *Friendship Groups*

_____A. Choosing friends on the basis of similar ethnic background threatens good group relations and divides our country. People should seek interethnic associations.

_____B. An individual should feel free, without a sense of guilt, to choose friends within his own ethnic group, or seek multiethnic contacts, or even change his ethnic identification if he desires.

_____C. People are better off, more comfortable, and safer when they stay within the bounds of their own ethnic group. They should seek friends from their own kind.

_____D. Other: _____
_____
_____

4. *Joining a Fraternity or Sorority*

_____A. Fraternities and sororities should be multiethnic so that the membership can learn to get along with all kinds of people.

_____B. Fraternities and sororities which do not have as their goal the preservation of religious or nationality values should be made open to all; those that are ethnically sponsored may place ethnic criteria for membership.

_____C. People should feel free to set up criteria in their social organizations any way they choose; this includes ethnic criteria.

_____D. Other: _____
_____
_____

5. *Interethnic Marriage*

_____A. Interethnic marriages are a good way to break down barriers between people and bring about a united America.

_____B. Interethnic marriages are a private affair between the couple involved, a matter of free choice if ethnic references mean little to them.

_____C. People are better off marrying within their own ethnic group; there are enough potentially good mates within one's own group.

_____D. Other: _____
_____
_____

6. *Voting for an Ethnic Candidate*

_____A. One should vote for the best candidate and not consider at all the candidate's ethnic background.

_____B. A voter who votes for a candidate from the same ethnic group as himself may be making sense if the candidate is qualified and takes a position that would serve the best interests of the voter and the group to which he belongs.

_____C. A voter should prefer a candidate from his own ethnic group since it is more likely that a candidate once in office would look out after the interests of the ethnic group.

_____D. Other: _____
_____
_____

7. *Ethnic Considerations for Appointments to Public Office* (Judges, etc.)

_____A. The choice of a person for a public office should rest solely on merit. Ethnic considerations are irrelevant.

_____B. Ethnic considerations do make sense when a large ethnic population resides in a voting area, yet has no representation on important governmental bodies.

_____C. An ethnic group should have the exact proportion of representatives in governmental bodies as its numbers in the voting population would indicate.

_____D. Other: _____

_____

_____

8. *Other-Nation Loyalties: Concern for Peoples outside the United States*

_____A. Concern with brethren overseas is narrow. One should be concerned with all people, how they are treated and whether they are suffering, not only with those with whom there are historic nationality ties.

_____B. Concern for overseas brethren seems natural, but the makers of foreign policy have to be guided by the self-interests of the nation, not the concerns of one group.

_____C. Americans who have historic ties to brethren overseas are the people who naturally will show the most concern. Exerting pressure on government officials is a democratic right of all Americans, and a democratic government which professes concern over the desires of its citizens must modify its foreign policy accordingly.

_____D. Other: _____

_____

_____

9. *Aid to Religious Schools*

———A. Religious schools help to separate people and prevent interethnic contact that makes for good human relations. All children should go to public schools.

———B. Religious schools are a democratic right, part of the exercise of
religious freedom, but they should be financed by their subscribers, not public funds.

———C. Parents should not be penalized for exercising their right to send
their children to religious schools. Since these schools meet
educational standards set by the state and provide the community's young people with a useful education, they should be
financed by public funds.

———D. Other: _____

_____

_____

Index

255